715 at 50

Henry Aaron addresses the capacity crowd on opening night.
(Randy Cox)

715 at 50

The Night Henry Aaron Changed Baseball and the World Forever

Text and Photos by Randy Louis Cox

SUMMER
GAME
BOOKS

Copyright © 2024 by Randy Louis Cox and Summer Game Books
Summer Game Books Edition Published March, 2024
All rights reserved.

No part of this publication may be reproduced, stored in a retrieval system, or transmitted in any form by any process – electronic, mechanical, photocopying, recording, or otherwise – without prior written permission from the copyright owner and the publisher. The scanning, uploading, and distribution of this book via the internet or any other means without the permission of the publisher is illegal.

ISBN: 978-1-955398-28-2 (paperback)
ISBN: 978-1-955398-29-9 (ebook)
ISBN: 978-1-955398-30-5 (hardcover)

For information about permission, bulk purchases, or additional distribution, write to

Summer Game Books
P. O. Box 818
South Orange, NJ 07079

or contact the publisher at www.summergamebooks.com

Randy Cox photographs copyright © *The Valley Times-News, Inc.,*
used with permission.

Major League Baseball trademarks and copyrights are used with permission of Major League Baseball. Visit MLB.com

Dedication

To our awesome grandchildren: Megan, Sarah, John, Brandon, Maddy, Austin, and Bradley, with love from Moondoggie and Mimi.

Acknowledgements

I couldn't have written this book about Henry Louis Aaron and the night he hit his 715th home run without assistance and encouragement from the following people:

Walt Friedman, publisher of Summer Game Books; Bob Hope, Ron Reed and Buzz Capra; Paul Crater and Jena Jones of the Atlanta History Center; Victor Sorrell, Doug Rowe and Susie Simmons; Adriana Pham of Major League Baseball; Sarit Babboni and Scott Cunningham of the Atlanta Braves; Daniel Evans, publisher of *The Valley Times-News*; Gary Black; my best friend, Paul Sharian; and, finally, to my lovely wife, Lanie Lessard-Cox, whose editing and proof-reading were indispensable.

About the Author

Randy Louis Cox was born in Atlanta, Georgia in 1950, and grew up in the nearby suburb of Decatur. He has been an editor, reporter, author, and award-winning photographer working in the field of journalism for 50 years.

715 at 50: The Night Henry Aaron Changed Baseball and the World Forever is his fourth book. Other books by Cox include:

- *A Baby Boomer's Guide to Collecting Comic Books and Baseball Cards,* published in 2004, Book I in the *Baby Boomer* collecting trilogy

- *Buying Back My Childhood* (2010), Book II, features chapters on collecting toys, board games, dolls, and action figures

- *It All Started with Davy Crockett* (2017) is the third volume, highlighting motion picture, television, Coca-Cola, and Disney collectibles.

He's been collecting since his dad and mother, Louis Purcell and Dahlia Sorrell Cox, gave him his first teddy bear, a Davy

Crockett outfit complete with Fess Parker coonskin cap, and a 1950s-era Disneyland *Frontierland* board game.

Cox retired from the Georgia Department of Agriculture in 2013 after 34 years of service, which included work in public relations and as assistant and then managing editor of *The Farmers and Consumers Market Bulletin*, a biweekly newspaper published by the Department.

Randy has worked in Georgia and Alabama as a reporter, area news and sports editor for several newspapers, and as a radio news broadcaster, as well as doing extensive public relations work.

He has performed freelance photography work for *Life Magazine* and received sixth place in the black-and-white photography competition at the Georgia National Fair in Perry, Georgia.

His articles and photographs of the equestrian events at the 1996 Atlanta Summer Olympic Games were published in the *Market Bulletin* when he was assistant editor there.

He and his wife, Lanie Lessard-Cox, share homes in Athens and Lilburn, Georgia.

Contents

Introduction – For the Love of Baseball, by Randy Louis Cox 3

Chapter One – 714 7

Chapter Two – Opening Night Arrives!............................ 17

Chapter Three – Henry Aaron's Long, Amazing Road to 715 23

Chapter Four – All-Star Lineup of Dignitaries 33

Chapter Five – Interview with Bob Hope, Former Braves' "Master of Public Relations" 53

Chapter Six – Henry Aaron and Me 65

Chapter Seven – Play Ball! The Game's Supporting Cast 75

Chapter Eight – Exclusive Interviews: Ron Reed & Buzz Capra 93

Chapter Nine – 715 101

Photo of Henry Aaron Hitting Home Run 715...........................106

Chapter Ten – Celebration Extraordinaire! 111

Chapter Eleven – True Greatness... 119

Chapter Twelve – A Hall of Fame Life....................................... 137

Bibliography.. 147

About the Photos

Among the highlights of *715 at 50* are 44 photographs author Randy Cox took the night Henry Aaron became major league baseball's all-time home run leader. Only a few of these have been published previously. To enrich the tribute to Henry Aaron and help tell a more complete story, the book also contains 22 photos from a variety of other sources.

The photos Randy took the night of April 8, 1974 all carry the photo credit "(Randy Cox)." One other photo bears that credit, that of the demolition of Atlanta Fulton-County Stadium, which the author snapped 23 years later.

The rest of the photos in the book come from a range of sources, and those are also identified by the credit that accompanies them. The Atlanta History Center was a valuable resource for several photos from earlier in Aaron's career and of his teammates; Major League Baseball provided permission to use images of Randy's Braves memorabilia, which enhances the story of the special relationship he had with Henry Aaron. And finally, several images were taken from the public domain.

Introduction
For the Love of Baseball

In 1957, Henry Louis Aaron, Eddie Mathews, and the rest of the Milwaukee Braves "roughnecks" (along with rival slugger Mickey Mantle of the hated New York Yankees) were without a doubt responsible for jump-starting my lifelong passion for baseball: watching, playing, reporting, writing, and taking 35-millimeter photographs, as shown in the pages of this collection from Aaron's BIG NIGHT: April 8, 1974, the evening that Hank vanquished the ghost of Babe Ruth and changed the national pastime and the world forever.

My following of The Hammer before he became The Hammer started in that long-ago season when he and the rest of the Braves upset the mighty Yankees in the World Series. As second-grade Cub Scouts, we watched the action on a lovely black-and-white television set in Decatur, Georgia, a suburb of Atlanta, during our weekly meeting, in an era when all World Series games were played in the afternoon. Webelo merit badges would just have to wait! We didn't know it at the time, but when Aaron came to bat, we were watching an Eagle Scout in action!

When Aaron passed away on January 22, 2021, I was heartbroken. He had been a part of my life since the glory days of the Milwaukee Braves as I watched his fantastic career unfold. The baseball world was saddened and stunned; he was such a great role model for youngsters and adults alike. He was not only a supremely talented player, but he was supremely dignified, never letting pressure or hatred or tremendous success change him.

The names of the great Braves' players on that Milwaukee team are music to my ears: Aaron and Mathews, Lew Burdette and Warren Spahn, Del Crandall and Joe Adcock, Frank Torre, Bill Bruton, Wes Covington, and Johnny Logan. Never could I have dreamed that 17 years after that World Series win I would have the privilege to cover Henry's most important baseball moment, a moment some believe to be the greatest in the history of sports.

Fast forward to the mid-1960s in Milwaukee, where forces were at work, unbeknownst to us kids, to bring Major League Baseball to the South—specifically, Atlanta. The wheels were in motion for the city to get its own Major League Baseball team, and it was going to be none other than my Braves. After a legal battle that kept the team in Milwaukee for one more year, Braves' Chairman of the Board William C. Bartholomay finally was able to relocate the team to Atlanta in 1966.

There was a drawback, however: the Braves were supplanting another of my beloved teams, the Atlanta Crackers, who were so successful they were sometimes referred to as "the Yankees of the South."

In 1971, I covered my first Braves game for a journalism class at Georgia State University in Atlanta. Luck was with me: Aaron hit his 600th home run that night, and my article appeared in the GSU *Signal* newspaper the next week. At the time, Aaron was only the third MLB player to reach that extraordinary plateau.

Three years later, as sports editor of *The Valley Times-News* in Lanett, Alabama, I applied for and received press and photography credentials from the Braves for myself and my cousin, Victor, whom I invited along for support. After we entered the

Introduction

Moments after hitting #715, Aaron is surrounded by teammates, family, and media—including me, off to the right (white arrow). (Floyd Jillson photographs, VIS 71.372.06, Kenan Research Center at Atlanta History Center.)

stadium, we stationed ourselves in the photographers' box near the home dugout for what would turn out to be the record-breaking night. Like every other photographer in the place, my goal was to take a photo of Aaron hitting THE home run.

Here is part of the story that I filed in the April 9, 1974, edition of the next afternoon's daily newspaper:

> *"An Atlanta stadium crowd of 53,775 gave The Hammer a standing ovation as he trotted around the bases. After he touched home plate, there was an 11-minute delay as Aaron went to be congratulated by his wife Billye, and parents, Mr. and Mrs. Herbert Aaron, Sr."*

Only a handful of us daily newspaper sports editors in Aaron's home state of Alabama (Mobile) covered this momentous event in person, as nearly all the major papers filed their stories using

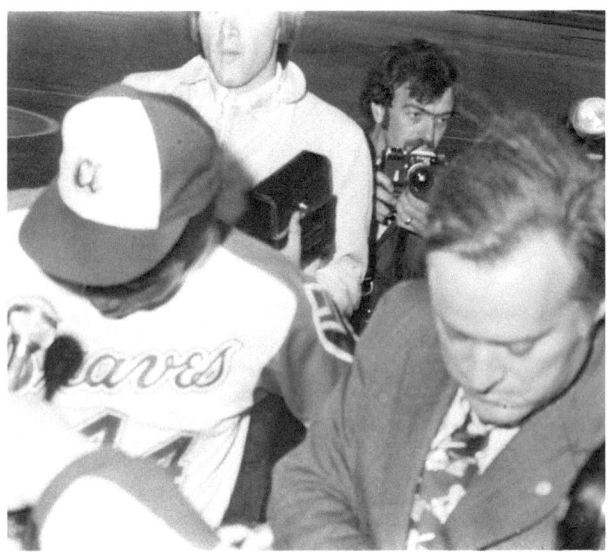

Henry in the crush of the media, including me, moments after he belted home run #715. (Randy Cox)

wire service copy and photos. Of course, no one knew if Aaron was going to hit Number 715 that night, but the excitement and anticipation were electric. For those of us who were there, it was unforgettable. What made it all the more incredible for me is, after the initial celebration with Aaron's family and teammates died down, The Hammer sat down for a moment to catch his breath. I quickly made a beeline over to my idol, shook his hand, and congratulated him. He nodded, and with a smile said "Thank you," a moment I've held close to me now for 50 years.

Randy Louis Cox

July, 2023

Chapter One
714

Henry Louis Aaron began the 1974 baseball season just one home run shy of tying George Herman (Babe) Ruth's record of 714. The Hammer was coming off a spectacular year in 1973, with a batting average of .301, 96 runs batted in, and leading the Atlanta Braves with 12 game-winning RBI's. He also collected his 40th homer in the next to the last game, joining Darrell Evans and Davey Johnson to make the Braves the first team in baseball history to have three players with 40 or more round trippers in one season. For a 39-year-old, it was an historically strong season, and considering the pressure Aaron was under, mind-boggling.

The Mobile, Alabama slugger started the 1973 season at a snail's pace, hitting only five home runs in April and batting a meager .125. He began to catch fire as July heated up the Atlanta nights, batting .324 with eight home runs. Then, in September, as he drew close to 715, Aaron went 28 for 66 (.426), with seven home runs, 21 RBI and 16 runs scored. He also collected six hits in the final two games, including #home run #713, to push his average for the season to .301, the 14th time in his career he surpassed the .300 mark. He also finished the season with 40 home runs in only 392 at bats, amazingly, at age 39 with the eyes of the world on him, the best seasonal rate of his career.

Henry's growing fame led to several lucrative endorsement contracts, like the one from Magnavox. (Author's Collection)

Part of Aaron's success was his mastery of hitting in the friendly confines of Atlanta Stadium, where in 64 games and 208 at-bats, he clobbered 24 home runs, drove in 55 runs, scored 45, and slugged .678. The Braves' move to Atlanta had made Aaron more of a pull hitter, and by this time of his career, he had elevated his batting technique to an art.

The opening game of the Braves' 1974 season was played on Thursday, April 4, at 2:30 PM at Riverfront Stadium, against the Reds. In fact, it was Major League Baseball's Opening Day, in an era when tradition still ruled and every season began with a day game in Cincinnati, in honor of the legendary Cincinnati Red Stockings of the 1860s. Vice-President Gerald Ford was in attendance to "pinch throw" the opening pitch for President Richard Nixon (who was busy with the Watergate scandal). Ford did not disappoint—tossing out two of them, one left-handed and the other right-handed!

The Reds' Pete Rose was ready for Hank to hit the ball his way in left field, saying that sometimes homers will hit the stadium's upper deck and bounce back on the field. "That is one ball I won't throw into the stands," he had joked.

If Aaron's 1973 40-homer season wasn't legendary enough, he wasted no time continuing his assault on Ruth's record, when on his first swing in the top of the first inning, ten minutes into the game, he launched a 3-and-1 sinker by right-hander Jack Billingham into the left-field stands for a three-run homer.

Well, Billingham's sinker didn't sink, and Aaron smashed it 400 feet over the 12-foot left-field wall. "You make a mistake on him, and it's gone," said Billingham later, a career 145-game winner and distant relative of Hall of Fame pitcher Christy Mathewson.

Clarence Williams, 22, a rookie patrolman with the Cincinnati Police Department and an off-duty security guard at Riverfront, snagged the home run ball on the first bounce. Williams, not thinking of personal gain (again, it was a different era), was anxious to present the ball to Aaron himself. Unfortunately for him, he was obligated to place it in a paper bag for an unidentified Reds' groundskeeper. Second-base umpire John McSherry took the ball from the bag, ran over to the Braves dugout, and gave it to Aaron.

Aaron had been swinging at special baseballs each time he came to the plate, ones marked to show indelible ink under ultraviolet light. After the 714th home run, the Braves announced that the ball used had been verified as the real thing: "14-1." Interestingly, for the 1974 season, MLB had decided to switch baseballs from a horsehide to cowhide cover, making Aaron's blast the first "cowhide long ball" in baseball history.

Horsehide to Cowhide

The announcement came in May 1973 from Baseball Commissioner Bowie Kuhn's office that beginning the next year, baseballs made from cowhide would be introduced in major league play alongside the traditional horsehide balls. Maybe horses in the U.S. were too busy starring in television shows and movies and couldn't be spared, but apparently there was a shortage of "quality" horsehide, and Rule 1.09 in the Official Baseball Rules was amended.

Baseball manufacturer Spalding Company of Massachusetts, whose baseballs were the only ones used in the majors at the time, had no problems with the new cowhide baseballs, but the players took a different viewpoint, saying that the cowhide balls were not stitched as tightly as horsehides, and were softer, meaning the ball would not carry as far. In 1976, the major leagues switched over to Rawlings Sporting Goods of Missouri to manufacture their baseballs, which continues to the present day.

Pittsburgh slugger Willie (Pops) Stargell had a "beef" with the cowhide balls, saying they tore easier than the others. Players were told if the covers came off the balls, "catch the cores." Stargell was a believer: his NL-leading production dropped by 19 homers in the '74 season. "Just about everybody was down (in homers)," he said. Henry Aaron smacked 20 long balls that year to end his career with the Braves.

Said Rules Chairman Johnny Johnson: color, texture, and resiliency for the cowhides made the "grade," having been utilized in batting practice and exhibition games.

After a kiss from his wife, Billye, and greetings from his parents, Herbert and Estella Aaron, Henry was congratulated in person by Ford, Kuhn, and Atlanta Braves owner Bill Bartholomay. As he took over the microphone, Aaron expressed the sentiment that he was "just glad it's almost over with."

It was hard to tell if Kuhn was there to see Aaron's home run or whether he wanted to observe opening day in the National League. Kuhn, Aaron was quoted as saying, was probably there for the latter.

At this point, Aaron was able to relax somewhat; he wasn't chasing anyone anymore. "It was like I had landed on the moon," he said. "But I've still got one more to go." Aaron was nearly as comfortable at Riverfront Stadium as he was at Fulton County, or it would seem, as overall he batted .336 there, with 11 home runs in 107 at-bats. He also collected his 3,000th hit there. Aaron also played his first major league game in Cincinnati, though that was at Crosley Field. He'll be forgiven for going 0-for-5 in his debut. For the record, he hit his first big league homer in his seventh game.

Billingham had already given up four homers to Hank (numbers 528, 636, 641, and 709) and complained about having to get new balls every time Aaron batted. New balls tend to be slicker, favoring the batter, as they are harder for pitchers to grip. Not only that, he wasn't happy with having to wait when time was called to honor Aaron in a six-minute ceremony for his 714th. "...seems to me they could have picked a better time to do it, like maybe between innings," he said.

Billingham had gotten very little sleep the night before the game, as deadly tornadoes swept through the area seven miles from where he and his family were living in Delhi, Ohio, a suburb of Cincinnati. The Cincy ace wasn't thinking about home runs... he was just trying to keep his family safe. "...there were things a heck of a lot more important to think about than home runs," he said. "...I didn't think about Hank or the home run all evening."

Luckily, no college students with a desire to jump onto the field were present, as the Vice President's Secret Service agents may have sprung into action.

The Reds received the consolation prize, as the Big Red Machine came back in the bottom of the 11th inning to beat the Braves 7-6. The only man to pitch in both the 714th and 715th games, Braves reliever Buzz Capra, was sent in to get the final out in the bottom of the 11th inning but didn't get it.

"I just wanted to save the game," he told me over the phone from Illinois during our interview (see chapter 8).

Capra's first batter was Pete Rose, who slammed a double to get things rolling. Next, Capra intentionally walked Joe Morgan. Cesar Geronimo was the next batter, and Capra threw a wild pitch that rolled way off into a corner outside of the dugout, as catcher Johnny Oates scrambled to retrieve it. Meanwhile, Rose was running all the way, and scored the winning run from second base on a walk-off.

Capra had watched from the Braves' dugout when Aaron tied the long-held record in the first inning.

"I was sitting there thinking about when I was in Little League, and now I'm in the big leagues, watching the man on my baseball cards," he added. "I was there when history was being made."

Capra ran on the field with the other players after Aaron's homer and patted him on the back, saying "Way to go, Hank, nice going, Hank."

"He wasn't a real rah, rah guy, but he was smiling and very happy," said Capra. "He was very relaxed, and we could see he was relieved."

Controversy soon developed between Kuhn and Braves Manager Eddie Mathews, as the skipper decided to sit Aaron for both the Saturday and Sunday games against the Reds to allow The Hammer a chance to break the record in front of the hometown fans in Atlanta-Fulton County Stadium. The teams had an off day on Friday and Aaron sat out Saturday. Kuhn told the Braves that there would be "serious penalties" if Aaron didn't play on Sunday. Without the Commissioner coming out and saying it, he certainly made it seem like suspensions might be in the on-deck circle. The previous year, Aaron had played an average of two out of three games, as Mathews wanted to rest him as much as possible, leaving it up to Aaron to determine if he felt strong enough to start the game.

Mathews was quoted as saying he was being dictated to by Kuhn who in turn was being handed marching orders by the New York City sportswriters. "The people in the southeast deserve to have the first opportunity to see the record broken," Mathews said.

Matthews yielded to Kuhn for the Sunday game, apparently the first time a player was thrown "into" a game instead of "out" of one. The Braves prevailed 5-3, behind a complete game victory by Phil Niekro, who went on to win 20 that season. Aaron went 0 for 3, as umpire John McSherry called him out on strikes twice against Reds hurler Clay Kirby.

Bowie Kuhn was baseball's fifth commissioner, holding the position for 15 years, from 1969–1984. (Public Domain).

"It's not that easy to hit a home run," Aaron said. "I wasn't guessing right. I was looking for a fastball and he (Kirby) threw me all sliders." After the game, the pitcher even said he thought he had gotten the benefit of a bad call on one of the strikeouts.

Braves officials, including Bartholomay and Braves public relations director Bob Hope, breathed collective sighs of relief because Henry would now have 11 games at home to break Ruth's record and the first date of the home stand, Monday, April 8, 1974, was coming up the next day. Like sugar plums at Christmas, visions of capacity crowds and record ticket sales at Atlanta Stadium danced in their heads.

It was projected by the Braves' accounting department that The Great Home Run Chase at home might be the difference between finishing the season in the black versus in the red. As it turned out, Aaron's otherworldly efficiency in breaking the record made it a short gravy train indeed.

The Aaron-Mathews-Kuhn tiff wasn't the only controversy that arose in the early days of the 1974 season: For Major League Baseball's Opening Day, occurring on the sixth anniversary of the assassination of Dr. Martin Luther King, Jr., Aaron had requested that there be a moment of silence in honor of Dr. King. But the Cincinnati Reds turned down the request. Later Aaron said the focus of the day should have been on King's legacy rather than Ruth's.

On a lighter note, Reds' catcher Johnny Bench was a big fan of The Hammer. In Mark Stewart and Mike Kennedy's 2006 book, *How the Media Made Henry Aaron Hammering Hank*, it described Bench as asking Henry to autograph a photo of him sliding safely under Bench's tag at home plate. "To John – Try to stay the h*** out of my way," Aaron signed.

Aaron for Commissioner

Henry Aaron's feud with Kuhn is well known in the annals of baseball lore, but fans might not be quite as familiar with the time The Hammer wanted to have his antagonist's job. As vice president and director of player development for the Atlanta Braves, Aaron in June 1983 expressed interest in the commissioner's job when the owners declined to renew Kuhn's contract. Aaron didn't accept the notion of some people who said he lacked qualifications for the position. "...Carter ran this country. He went from being a peanut farmer to running the White House," he said. However, he wasn't hired, as owners sought someone who would be more focused on business than baseball, and hired Peter Ueberroth, who had engineered the hugely successful 1984 Summer Olympics in Los Angeles.

Aaron greeted by manager and long-time ally, Eddie Mathews. (Randy Cox)

Chapter Two
Opening Night Arrives!

Back in Atlanta, on Monday, April 8, 1974, anticipation reached to the heavens and back as Henry Aaron would have his first opportunity to smash Ruth's cherished mark, the one fans and baseball purists called "the record that will never be broken." As it was the Braves' home opener, it was a double celebration. Preparations were extensive and festivities were about to begin for what would turn out to be one of baseball's most historic nights.

As a rookie sports editor for *The Valley Times-News* in Lanett, Alabama, I was thrilled to be heading to Georgia with my cousin Victor to cover the game. My thoughts heading into Atlanta-Fulton County Stadium could be described as "excited anticipation," not knowing if this would be THE NIGHT. Although I was filled with confidence in The Hammer, I was also realistic: It's just not that easy to hit a home run, especially with the eyes of the world upon him. I found out later that he "called his shot" by telling teammates Ralph Garr and Dusty Baker that he was going to "get it over with tonight." As we showed our press passes and entered the photographers' box, Victor told me he was going to catch a foul ball during the game. And he did! Talk about an amazing night!

My main concern was trying to get us a good spot to take some great black-and-white photos. As we were setting up, a heated discussion broke out between me and a local newspaper photographer who told me that camera space was a "universal problem" and that I needed to move away from "his space." I didn't know it at the time, but we were entitled to be in our spot since PR man Hope's policy was first come, first served. And we were there first! Luckily, a friendly gentleman wearing a cowboy hat told us we could slide into the space next to him. Professional courtesy was NOT dead! We were all happy and we completely ignored the newspaper lensman for the rest of the night. We had a great spot for the action and could exit quickly onto the field to get close to the pregame fun that was about to begin. Incidentally, as Hope explained to me later, I wasn't the only photographer who had space problems.

All the trappings for a major event were in place. Bob Hope and his staff had done their usual great job in getting things ready, and everyone in the stands was chomping at the bit for the pregame festivities to begin. Reporters were busy, furiously writing their copy in the press box and elsewhere, and photographers, including myself, were on the field snapping photos of Braves and Dodgers players, celebrities, and baseball officials.

The team had hired 44 batgirls (all wearing Aaron's number 44 on their jerseys), who formed a gauntlet on the field to usher in Mr. Aaron on his special night, as his teammates gathered nearby for a gala celebration in his honor.

By game time, there were a total of 400 reporters and photographers who had obtained press passes for the big event. Some of them were in photographer boxes, others in the press box, while still more were stationed in the upper decks behind the outfield positions.

In the first-base box where we were ensconced, there must have been about 15 photographers, most of us with a couple of 35-mm cameras, strobes, and telephoto lenses. Everyone wanted to get as many snaps as possible, with the pressure building to incredible heights in anticipation of Aaron coming to the plate. I used

Opening Night Arrives!

Festivities commence for one of the greatest nights in baseball history as 44 batgirls await Henry Aaron's appearance. (Randy Cox)

a state-of-the-art Minolta single-lens-reflex camera, having been trained on it only a year previously by my chief photographer Doug Rowe, who so expertly cropped the printed photos that I took for the newspaper. I used my 200-mm telephoto lens to catch all the action on the field, but for closeups, I went back to my regular 50 millimeter. Even 50 years later, the negatives of the photos are sharp and clear when converted into digital scans.

As batgirls prepared themselves for arrival of the Man of the Hour, maintenance crews performed last-minute preparations to make sure the field at Atlanta-Fulton County Stadium was in immaculate condition. The $18-million hitter-friendly stadium was constructed in the record-breaking time of 51 weeks in 1964-65, but the Braves had to wait an extra year for their new home due to litigation that held them in Milwaukee.

Batgirls and the Braves' maintenance crew get ready for the big moment. (Randy Cox)

Unhappily for Atlanta fans, in the first regular season game in Atlanta on April 12, 1966, the Pittsburgh Pirates edged the debuting Braves, 3-2, as slugger Willie Stargell crunched the winning home run in the 13th inning. He said he didn't think Tony Cloninger's (who pitched all 13 innings!) curve ball would go out. "It wasn't hit too well," he said. At the time, the Pirates' hitters believed this was not a good home run park, complaining that the ball didn't carry well there. However, their opinion changed quickly about the new three-tiered, concrete stadium.

The only consolation for Henry Aaron was that he stole the first base ever in a regular season game at the stadium, and it was a clutch one, after hitting a lead-off single in the bottom of the 11th.

**

Besides providing festive decorations for Atlanta Stadium, security was beefed up as 60-plus police officers were in attendance. In the left-field bleachers where Number 715 was predicted to land, six officers, four or five undercover security men and eight additional ushers were stationed there to insure against a battle that could break out if the ball were to land there.

From the photographers' box, we could feel a kind of magical excitement emanating from the record-breaking crowd of 53,775 fans anxiously awaiting Henry Aaron's grand entrance onto the field through a phalanx of batgirls happily waiting to greet him. He would be escorted by Braves radio and television personality, Milo Hamilton. It was not known if the native Iowan had been rehearsing his signature home run calls of "Holy Cow!" and "Holy Toledo!" in anticipation of Aaron hitting number 715, but he probably did.

Milo had begun broadcasting major league games for the St. Louis Browns (1953), then moving to the Cardinals (1954), Cubs (1956-57 and 1980-84), White Sox (1962-65), Braves (1966-75), Pirates (1976-79) and Astros (1985-2012).

Former Milwaukee Braves pitcher Ernie Johnson and broadcaster Larry Munson, famous for calling the University of Georgia football games ("sugar falling from the sky"), were the color commentators in the booth with Milo during the Braves' early years in Atlanta.

Aaron entered the field with Hamilton at his side, sending the crowd into a frenzy. When the deafening roar died down and the fans settled back into their seats, Aaron finally got his chance to speak. He was a long way from his early minor league days in Jacksonville, FL and Eau Claire, WI, yet the cool collectedness he possessed surely had been part of his persona back then too, and had given him the strength to persevere and reach the present moment.

The focus of the entire world was on him, and he responded in his own unflappable and modest way...as he always did. His

Hammerin' Hank arrives with Milo Hamilton as the crowd goes wild! (Randy Cox)

career had been remarkable, compiling mind-boggling batting numbers against the likes of Sandy Koufax, Bob Gibson, Tom Seaver, Don Drysdale, Gaylord Perry, Robin Roberts, Juan Marichal, not to mention dozens of other challenging hurlers. And he had done so with almost machine-like consistency over 20 seasons, earning the respect of his teammates and opponents alike. It was not until Aaron began his assault on Babe Ruth's total of 714 home runs that many fans became aware of his greatness.

Chapter Three

Henry Aaron's Long, Amazing Road to 715

During his junior year in high school, Aaron played semi-pro baseball for the Mobile Black Bears, and when the Indianapolis Clowns (the "Globetrotters of Baseball") played the Bears at the end of the season, the Indy team was so interested they ponied up a $200-a-month contract for Aaron to sign. For years, the southern Alabama area had been a hotbed for baseball talent.

Aaron enjoyed some early positive press coverage when he played for the barnstorming Clowns. *The Pittsburgh Courier*, a Black newspaper, wrote, "Henry Aaron has been the shining light for the Funmakers in the early games. His batting and fielding have been a revelation." Aaron was familiar with revelation, but only in the Bible.

"Major league scouts are swarming to parks where the Clowns are playing to get a good look at the young Aaron," wrote *The Chicago Defender* newspaper. "All seem to agree that he stands at the plate like a Ted Williams."

Aaron drew most attention from two big-league clubs, the Milwaukee Braves and New York Giants. The Wisconsin team won the bidding war (by $200), signing him to a whopping $350-per-month contract. Beginning in the Braves' farm system in Class C Eau Claire, Wisconsin, he was voted to the Northern League All-Star Team and the league's Most Outstanding Rookie in 1952.

No dark clouds for The Hammer. (Randy Cox)

However, don't feel sorry for the Giants. They already had a guy named Willie Mays! What an outfield pair they would have made!

Shortstop Aaron had started off batting cross-handed, and while coaches tried to correct it, he STILL made a good impression at the plate. Aaron hit .336 as an 18-year-old for the Braves' Class C team in Eau Claire, Wisconsin, striking out only 19 times in nearly 400 plate appearances.

Next stop on the road to the majors was Jacksonville, where he met his first wife, Barbara Lucas, sister of Bill Lucas, future Atlanta Braves' executive. Aaron played second base with the

Jacksonville Braves of the Class A South Atlantic League. He played for the man who turned out to be his favorite manager, Ben Geraghty, who was quoted as saying Henry never saw a pitcher he couldn't hit. Ben eventually won three pennants for Jacksonville before passing away June 18, 1963.

Aaron led Jax to the pennant and was named the league's Most Valuable Player, receiving 75 percent of the vote. He batted .362, along with 22 homers, 125 RBI, and 115 runs scored in just 137 games. Along with teammates Horace Garner and Felix Mantilla, he and two black players from Savannah, Al Israel and Fleming Reedy, were the first five players to break the color barrier in the Sally League.

Right-fielder Garner injured his knee in 1953, sidetracking his chances for making it in the Majors with the Braves. Aaron commented that Horace had "one of the strongest throwing arms" he'd ever seen.

Mantilla, who also later played for the Milwaukee Braves, helped ruin a perfect game on May 26, 1959, for Pittsburgh Pirates' Harvey Haddix in the 13th inning by grounding to third baseman Don Hoak, who threw wildly to first base, and Felix reached on the error. Sportswriters of the day said that left-hander Haddix turned in the greatest pitching performance in baseball history, an event that is highlighted in the National Baseball Hall of Fame in Cooperstown, New York. After 12 perfect innings, Haddix lost in the 13th on a Joe Adcock double. Lou Burdette went the distance for the Braves, allowing 10 hits.

Harvey ("Kitten") Haddix could only say, "It's just another loss – and they're not good."

In 1954, Aaron came close to being sent to the Atlanta (to play for the Crackers), 12 years before he arrived as a member of the Milwaukee Braves in 1966. That spring it was expected that he would play for the Crackers, where he would have broken the color barrier in the Southern League. But fate had other ideas.

The 20-year-old, having been switched from shortstop and second base to the outfield, also had been pegged to play for the Braves' AAA Toledo farm team, but that didn't transpire either as he was elevated to the major leagues to substitute for Bobby ("Shot Heard 'Round the World") Thomson, who had fractured his ankle sliding into second base on March 13. Filling Thomson's roster spot, Aaron, in his first Grapefruit League start the next day against the Boston Red Sox, rapped out three hits, including a moon-shot home run.

Aaron himself broke his ankle on September 5, 1954, and, ironically, Thomson went in to run for him. Hank finished fourth in the balloting for Rookie of the Year, an award captured by Wally Moon of the Cardinals. Ernie Banks (Cubs) and Gene Conley, Aaron's teammate, finished second and third, respectively.

Roy Campanella, Hall of Famer and one of the greatest catchers in MLB history with Brooklyn, looked admiringly at Aaron in his early years with the Braves. Aaron's "gonna be murder on us in a couple of years. He's a natural swinger, and I don't think a pitcher's gonna be able to find a weak spot on him once he gets a little more experience."

After a solid sophomore season in which Aaron batted .314 with 27 home runs and 106 runs batted in, his career took full bloom in his third year in the league, in 1956, when he won his first batting title and was recognized by *The Sporting News* as the National League Player of the Year.

The next season, he captured the National League Most Valuable Player Award, nearly winning the Triple Crown with 44 home runs, 132 runs batted in, and a batting average of .322. He was all of 23.

On September 23, 1957, in a game against the St. Louis Cardinals, Aaron smacked an 11th-inning walk-off home run off Billy Muffet to clinch a World Series berth for the Braves.

"All I could think of as I rounded the bases was Bobby Thomson's home run in 1951," Aaron said following the victory. "The one that won the playoff game for the Giants over Brooklyn."

"The last time I faced him, he (Muffet) threw me a fastball on the first pitch, so I was looking for a curve," Aaron said. He added that when he hit it, he knew he had hit it well.

Against the Pinstripe Boys in the series, Aaron and third baseman Mathews provided the firepower at the plate, and series MVP Lew Burdette (three wins) and Warren Spahn (one win) combined to pitch the underdog "Bushville" Braves to victory in seven games. Burdette had to pitch Game 7 on only two days' rest, as Spahn contracted the flu. Amazingly, Burdette came through with his second consecutive shutout.

For the 10 years between 1953 and 1962, Spahn and Burdette won an amazing 372 games, or nearly 19 per season each. The story goes that Burdette learned how to pitch during World War II by throwing rocks at an abandoned munitions plant.

Spahn is certainly one of the greatest pitchers of all time, and perhaps the greatest left-hander. "Spahn and Sain and pray for rain" wasn't just an idle slogan. Spahn led the NL in complete games nine times, and in victories eight times. He won 20 games or more 13 times and had 100 or more strikeouts for 17 straight years. He won 363 games (356 for the Braves), an all-time high for lefthanders.

Arkansas native Sain won 100 games for the Boston Braves before being traded to the Yankees for Lew Burdette and

$50,000. Sain became a valuable and versatile pitcher for the Yanks for several years before becoming a highly acclaimed pitching coach. Sain was also an exceptional hitter, fanning only 20 times in his career in more than 850 plate appearances!

The '57 championship game lasted two hours and thirty-four minutes as fans in Milwaukee and around the country watched the afternoon game on black-and-white television sets from their homes, appliance stores, and bars.

An employee in Milwaukee's Piccadilly Bar said there was nothing but silence from the fans until the bottom of the ninth inning. "When Mathews made that play, I thought the joint had exploded," he said. "I've never seen anything like that celebration, and I don't think I ever will."

The Braves secured the National League pennant for the second straight year in 1958, finding themselves in the series against the Yanks again, but this time, no dice, as the Pinstripe Crew prevailed, powered by a healthy Mickey Mantle and home run hitting by Hank Bauer, who went deep four times.

Two words come to mind when thinking of Henry Louis Aaron's career: persistence and longevity. The 1960s was a banner decade for The Hammer, as he spent six years in Milwaukee the first part of the decade, and the four remaining in Atlanta. He clobbered home run #200 off Ron Kline (St. Louis Cardinals) on July 3, 1960; #300 off Roger Craig (New York Mets) on April 19, 1963; #400 off Bo Belinsky (Philadelphia Phillies) on April 20, 1966; and #500 off Mike McCormick (San Francisco Giants) on July 14, 1968—four home run milestones in one decade!

And what a decade it was for The Hammer: he scored over 100 runs every year from 1960-69 except for the 84 he scored in 1968. His total was 1,091 runs scored in that period. Henry also collected 1,107 runs batted in. And, he finished with 375 home runs, hitting 40 or more homers five seasons. When he turned 35 in 1970, he STILL had six more good years with the Braves and Milwaukee Brewers. Consistent, long-lasting excellence allowed Aaron to produce career numbers matched by few in the history of the game.

Interestingly, Bad Henry found an unexpected way to bring in some extra money after the 1959 season was over. As a participant in the television program "Home Run Derby," filmed in Los Angeles and pitting two power-hitting ballplayers in head-to-head competition to see who could hit the most home runs in a nine-inning "game," Hank was in his element. His competition was formidable: Eddie Mathews, Al Kaline, Duke Snider, Bob Allison, Jim Lemon, Ken Boyer, and Wally Post. He faced teammate Mathews in a 1960 contest, winning 4-3 with a home run in the bottom of the ninth inning.

Anything hit other than a home run was considered an "out." Aaron discovered that HR hitters make the "big money," as he carried away $30,000 in winnings and collected the most homers overall in the competition. He only garnered a $17,000 salary the same year. With his winnings, the unselfish Aaron bought his parents a grocery store in Toulminville, Alabama.

The year 1970 was a great one for Aaron. In a May 17 game, he beat out an infield grounder for his 3,000th career hit. He was later honored for this achievement on "Hank Aaron Day," May 26, 1971. For his efforts, he was given a golf cart with the number "44" inscribed on it, a year's supply of Coca-Cola, and a French poodle. He gave his most prized possession at the time, the 3,000th hit ball, to the National Baseball Hall of Fame, but apparently it was put in storage and not on display when it first arrived.

Henry savors the moment, surrounded by (L-R) Andrew Young, Ernie Johnson, wife Billye, and Governor Jimmy Carter. (Randy Cox)

Hank's 3001st hit was a home run, as was Stan Musial's in 1958. The Hammer had joined some elite company when he entered the 3,000-hit club: Musial (1958), Paul Waner (1942), Eddie Collins and Tris Speaker (1925), Ty Cobb (1921), Nap Lajoie and Honus Wagner (1914), and Cap Anson (1897).

In his years with the Milwaukee Braves, Aaron blasted more home runs on the road than he did at County Stadium (203 to 195). Once the team moved that trend was reversed, as with the friendlier dimensions and thinner air in Atlanta, Aaron turned himself into much more of a pull hitter beginning in 1966.

Aaron was elected to the Baseball Hall of Fame in 1982 with 97.83 per cent of the vote. Fellow inductees that August were Frank Robinson, MLB's first Black manager; Travis Jackson of the New York Giants; and Albert Benjamin (Happy) Chandler, Sr., the second commissioner of baseball.

Currently in the baseball museum, Henry Louis Aaron is one of only two players (Babe Ruth is the other one) who has his own exhibit. It's called "Chasing the Dream," and opened in 2009, chronicling his life story from the early beginnings and major league career to his humanitarian efforts after he retired from baseball. Artifacts include the bat and ball from home run 714, tying Babe Ruth; his 755th home run ball; bats and balls from his 500th and 600th home runs, and his 3,000th hit; his 1957 World Series ring and MVP award; and the uniform he wore when he broke the Bambino's record. On loan from the Atlanta Braves is his 715th HR bat and ball. "If you consider what he means to this country, not just baseball fans, it's a fitting tribute," said a Hall of Fame spokesman. When Aaron pledged to donate his collection for the Chasing the Dream exhibit, he said it was "the proudest moment of my life." With the astronomical value of such items today, some players might instead auction off their memorabilia "for their family" or kept it in their own possession.

Henry Aaron was honored in his hometown of Mobile, Alabama in 1997, as the home of the minor league Mobile Bay Bears was named Hank Aaron Stadium or "The Hank." It's located at the corner of Satchel Paige Drive and Bolling Brothers Boulevard. The Bay Bears took on the Birmingham Barons in the first game at the new field. The Bears ended their franchise run on September 2, 2019.

Chapter Four
All-Star Lineup of Dignitaries

On the magical night of April 8, 1974, the sidelines were a virtual *Who's Who* of prominent Atlanta politicians, major league baseball executives, and some of the biggest African-American names in the entertainment industry.

In attendance was Atlanta Mayor Maynard Holbrook Jackson, Jr., elected the city's first Black mayor in 1973, serving three terms. His name was added to Hartsfield Atlanta International Airport in 2003, and in 2012 the airport's new international terminal was named for him. In 1968, the 30-year-old Jackson ran against Sen. Herman Talmadge (D-Ga.) for the U.S. Senate, losing the election but gaining much support from the Black community.

Georgia governor James Earl (Jimmy) Carter Jr., also present to see Aaron's big home run, was the 39th president of the United States, from 1977 to 1981. This night, he was Georgia's 76th governor (1971-75). Since retiring from the presidency, Carter received the Nobel Peace Prize for his humanitarian work, which includes Habitat for Humanity and countless other endeavors.

During the post-home run #715 celebration, Carter presented Henry Aaron with his own personal license plate, "HENRY – 715," stating the slugger had done as much to "rehabilitate" the city and "legitimize" the South as any person.

VIPs, L-R: Eddie Robinson, Maynard Jackson, Jimmy Carter, Andrew Young, and Ivan Allen, Jr. (Randy Cox)

Ambassador Andrew Jackson Young, Jr. was elected mayor of Atlanta in 1981 with 55 percent of the vote, following in the footsteps of trailblazer Jackson. Young was instrumental in the renovation of Zoo Atlanta following re-election with 80 percent of the vote for a second term in 1985. In 1977, President Carter appointed Young to serve as the first African-American ambassador to the United Nations.

Former Mayor Ivan Earnest Allen Jr., who served two terms as Atlanta mayor during the height of the Civil Rights Movement, was also in attendance.

Allen was also instrumental in drawing in the new franchise Atlanta Falcons (football) and the Atlanta Chiefs (soccer), both in 1967, and the Atlanta Hawks (from St. Louis, basketball) in 1968.

Atlanta Braves General Manager William Edward (Eddie) Robinson, a former major league first baseman for seven American League teams, was there. Robinson became the oldest living former player in 2019 before he passed away on October 4, 2021, at the age of 100.

Robinson's 13-year career began in 1942 but was interrupted by service in World War II. His return in 1946 saw him become a four-time All-Star, hitting 172 career home runs, and winning a World Championship with the Cleveland Indians in 1948. Legend Ted Williams once called him the "best clutch hitter" he ever played against.

Popular vocalist Pearl Bailey, who in 1976 became the first African American to receive the Screen Actors Guild (SAG) Lifetime Achievement Award, sang the "Star-Spangled Banner" at Henry's request before the game began. In the excitement of the evening, she hoped to remember the words, she related. Ms. Bailey was awarded the Presidential Medal of Freedom in 1988.

Pearl was the subject of an interview before the game by *The Atlanta Constitution*'s Wayne Minshew, the first Braves beat reporter for the morning paper. Minshew studied journalism at the University of Georgia, Athens, while having a successful collegiate pitching career, setting a record 1.02 earned run average as the Bulldogs' captain. Later, he became the Braves' director of public relations.

By this time in Henry Aaron's life, he and his wife Barbara had divorced.

In 1973's off-season, Hank and Billye Williams were married at the University of the West Indies chapel in Mona, Jamaica. Billye had become in 1968 the first African American woman in the South to co-host a daily hour-long talk show when she was hired by Atlanta's WSB-TV for *Today in Georgia.*

Born in Anderson County, Texas on October 16, 1936, to Nathan and Annie Mae Smith Suber, Billye graduated from

Singer Pearl Bailey, with a glossy of Aaron in hand, holds court with Bartholomay (center) and Braves beat reporter Wayne Minshew (with notepad). (Randy Cox)

Lincoln High School in Dallas, Texas in 1954. She received a Bachelor of Arts degree in English from Texas College in Tyler, Texas, along with a Master of Arts degree in 1960 from Atlanta University.

Mrs. Aaron taught school in the Atlanta Public School System and at Morris Brown College, South Carolina State, Morehouse College, and Spelman College.

Her other achievements include hosting a weekly talk show, "Billye," for WTMU-TV; working with the United Negro College Fund (UNCF) in Atlanta, as the development director; and founding the Mayor of Atlanta's MASKED Ball.

Billye Aaron was also named director emeritus of the Legal Defense Fund for the National Association for the Advancement of Colored People (NAACP).

Billye Aaron (left) awaits the start of the game. (Randy Cox)

Billye retired in 1994, as she and her husband began the Hank Aaron Chasing the Dream Foundation which assists low-income children in receiving scholarships.

She also received the 2003 Martin Luther King, Jr. "Salute to Greatness" Award; the YWCA Woman of Achievement Award; the Southern Christian Leadership Conference (SCLC) Seventh Annual Martin Luther King, Jr. Memorial Drum Major for Justice Award; the Atlanta Urban League's 1998 Distinguished Community Service Award; and the Atlanta Anti-Defamation League of B'nai B'rith Abe Goldstein Human Relations Award.

In 1973, Hank and Billye appeared on the "Dinah Shore Television Show," and the couple even sang "Stars Fell on Alabama," after some encouragement by their host. The new groom appeared solo on several other TV shows that winter, hosted by Mike Douglas, David Frost, Merv Griffin, and Flip Wilson, where he did a comedy sketch in which Wilson refused to sell baseball equipment to Aaron for $7.13. "Would you settle for 713?" Wilson asked The Hammer.

Celebrity Box: "Miss Lillian" and Rosalynn Carter, seated in back, and in front of them, Sammy Davis, Jr. and wife Altovise.
(Randy Cox)

Sitting in a first-base field box were singer/actor Sammy Davis, Jr., and his wife Altovise. An all-around entertainer of "Rat Pack" fame, Sammy offered $25,000 to Aaron for the 715th ball, but it wasn't for sale! Seated with them were "Miss Lillian" Carter, Jimmy Carter's mother, and Rosalyn Carter, Jimmy's wife. I wish I had taken the time to speak to these notables, but there was just too much going on!

Other celebrities in attendance were TV personality Redd Foxx ("Sanford and Son"); former college and National Football League Coach Bill Curry and his wife, Carolyn; author George Plimpton, a pioneer in participatory journalism; National League President Chub Feeney; and Monte Irvin, promotion assistant to Baseball Commissioner Bowie Kuhn. Prominent by his absence at Atlanta-Fulton County Stadium that night was Kuhn, who opted instead to attend a dinner in Cleveland.

"Who's hitting 715 in Cleveland tonight?" the Braves' front-office man, Donald Davidson, asked.

"Phooey on Bowie"

Some not-too-flattering signs draping Atlanta Stadium from fans directed at his employer, Bowie Kuhn, greeted Monte Irvin as he arrived too late for the pregame ceremony: "Did King Kuhn OK the Lineup?" "Send Kuhn to the Moon," "Hank 715, Kuhn 0," and "Phooey on Bowie." Monte may have been thinking that it was going to be a very long night indeed.

A former resident of East Orange, New Jersey, where he collected 16 letters in high school, Monte Irvin started off his baseball career with the Newark, N.J. Eagles of the Negro National League before he got his big break with the New York Giants in 1949. His career, interrupted by an Army stint during World War II, took off when he helped power the Giants to the National League pennant in 1951 and World Series three years later. He hit .293 in seven seasons, highlighted by a .329 year in 1953.

Irvin was a three-time Negro Leagues batting champion before reaching the majors at age 30. (Public Domain)

> Elected to the Baseball Hall of Fame in 1981 by the Committee on Negro Leagues, Irvin was sent to Atlanta by Kuhn to represent the commissioner's office.
>
> After being the target of boos and catcalls from Atlanta fans, Irvin acknowledged that Kuhn should have been there, not him. Kuhn said he was absent not because he was afraid of being heckled by the hometown crowd, but because he had received two invitations that night: one to Atlanta Stadium and the other to a Wahoo Club banquet in Cleveland. Said Kuhn, "Since I had been in Cincinnati with Hank when he hit his historic 714th home run, I felt it was appropriate for me to be here" in Cleveland.

The 30-minute pregame festivities were elaborate and exciting, featuring a *This is Your Life* show for Henry Aaron in center field, where there was a huge American flag shaped like the United States. Gathered were relatives, friends, former managers, teammates, and celebrities to highlight various parts of Aaron's life.

Henry's parents, Herbert and Estella, stood on the state of Alabama, where Aaron grew up in the Down the Bay community, while the Braves' John Mullen, who signed Henry from the Indianapolis Clowns, was placed on Indiana, and Traveling Secretary Donald Davidson settled on Boston, Massachusetts where The Hammer first signed with the Boston Braves in, 1952. Charlie (Jolly Cholly) Grimm, his first big league manager, was situated on Wisconsin.

Other pregame activities included the singing of the 1900 spiritual hymn, "Lift Every Voice" (Aaron's favorite) by the Morris

Brown College Choir of Atlanta; a musical presentation from the Jonesboro, Georgia High School Marching Band; and the ceremonial first pitch thrown out by Hank's father.

Henry was one of eight children raised by the elder Aarons. When Henry was a boy, Herbert operated farm machinery and worked as a boilermaker's assistant/riveter on a coal barge to support his family. Toulminville, the town where they lived, was known as "Strangleville," as it was a very poor area, where residents sometimes found it hard to pay their rent.

When Herbert came home from that job at the Alabama Dry Dock and Shipbuilding Company (ADDSCO) in the evening, he enjoyed sharing his love of the National Pastime with his eager son, Hank, telling him that when he was a child he had seen Babe Ruth play in an exhibition game in Mobile.

Herbert said Hank was "crazy about playing baseball." "I couldn't keep a ball out of his hands," but said that he never dreamed his son would reach the heights of the "greatest record in baseball." The elder Aaron would throw his son bottle caps and let him smack them with a broom handle, helping his son to develop quick hands and great hand-eye coordination. As a young man, in the days of iceboxes, Henry also delivered ice, which he credited as a reason for his powerful wrists.

In his early teens, Henry was able to see his hero, Jackie Robinson, play with the Brooklyn Dodgers in an exhibition game, and related to his dad he hoped he could make it to the major leagues before Robinson retired.

Hank said he gave his father credit for "the little bitty things he said," to bolster his career. Herbert passed away May 21, 1998, at the age of 89.

His mother Estella said of Henry, "when he's feeling good, it's just too bad for the pitchers." All his home runs have been great "like they should be for a momma."

Estella passed away on April 7, 2008, in an Atlanta hospital, at the age of 96.

Henry and Bill Bartholomay. (Randy Cox)

Braves Chairman of the Board William C. (Bill) Bartholomay was instrumental in bringing the Milwaukee Braves to Atlanta in 1966, when it was unlikely anyone in the Braves' new hometown, nor even Aaron himself, imagined eight short years later they would be observing Aaron's pursuit of immortality.

A native of Lake Forest, Illinois, about 45 minutes from Chicago, Bartholomay worked in the family insurance business, building it into one of the largest brokerage firms in the city. According to Braves publications, Bill bought Stevens Candy Kitchens of Chicago with a friend.

"The company thrived and became a shining example of what Bill Bartholomay can do," an article stated. "He used it as a steppingstone to greater things. He and two other men developed an idea that would allow people to send candy as easily as a telegram." That brainchild eventually morphed into Western Union's "Candygram."

In 1961, he became part of an 11-man consortium that purchased an interest in the Chicago White Sox. He sold that venture, and with several other investors, bought a controlling interest in the Milwaukee Braves. A contentious legal battle against city and county governments in Milwaukee followed his expression that he wished to move the team to Atlanta.

In his autobiography, Donald Davidson had some thoughts on the Braves' shift from Milwaukee to Atlanta. Davidson was well qualified to comment, having worked for the franchise in all three cities. He cited dropping attendance numbers, a lack of interest in public funding, and the potential of the large, untapped market of the South. Also, Milwaukee was not a major population center and faced competition from the two Chicago teams and the recent arrival of the Washington Senators, who had become the Minnesota Twins.

After Atlanta was picked as the new host city, the city and county of Milwaukee filed a lawsuit to keep the team at County Stadium for one more year, causing the Braves to endure a "lame duck year" before relocating in 1966.

Houston Horn of *Sports Illustrated* wrote: "The speed of the wheels was highly reminiscent of the noise in Boston 12 years ago when the Braves pulled out for Milwaukee."

When the team finally left Milwaukee, it was the first time a major league squad had left a city that had no other franchise. The Atlanta Crackers, kings of the Southern and International

Leagues, played at Atlanta Stadium as an IL team in 1965 following demolition of its own home, Ponce de Leon Ballpark, where the storied franchise in one stretch won championships in 10 out of 12 seasons. The Earl Mann-owned Crackers had many famous alumni, including Luke Appling, Chuck Tanner, Bob Uecker, Tim McCarver, Bob Montag, and Eddie Mathews.

Standing four feet tall and weighing 85 pounds, Donald Davidson had a bout with sleeping sickness as a youngster, which stunted his growth. At nine years old, he started out as a bat boy with the Boston Braves, moving right up the ladder to public relations director, traveling secretary, game director, assistant to the president and assistant to the chairman, as the team moved to Milwaukee and then Atlanta.

Known for his practical jokes, Davidson had the tables turned on him in 1957 when he became the world's smallest streaker. The cover story of the *1974 Braves Scorebook* relates the tale of Don posing for a team photograph in the outfield of Milwaukee County Stadium. Following the conclusion of the photo shoot, pitchers Spahn and Burdette, along with Mathews, wrestled the little guy's clothes off, and Don "streaked" to the dugout in front of several thousand fans—or so the legend goes. Not one to let this go by, he retaliated by soaking Spahn's clothes in the whirlpool (or shower depending on which version you believe). The winningest left-hander had a lot of trouble getting into his clothes that night.

If Davidson was baseball's first streaker, the second one may have come during Aaron's 714th home run game in Cincinnati. It featured the shocking appearance of a teenager who disrobed and ran through the bleachers amongst the fans. He was taken into custody.

In Davidson's 1972 autobiography, *Caught Short*, he related another prank aimed at him...this one occurring at the Netherland Hilton Hotel in Cincinnati at 2 in the morning. Again, Burdette and Spahn were the antagonists as the little man hopped on the hotel elevator to return to his room on the 26th floor. The pitchers themselves were roommates on the 11th floor, and upon reaching it, Donald asked them to punch 26. "Punch it yourself, you little so-and-so," they said, or some words to that effect, before stepping off at their floor. Davidson angrily traveled back down to the lobby, snagging a bellhop to punch the correct button for him. Thinking ahead, Donald solved this problem the next time by moving the team to a hotel with fewer stories.

Donald enjoyed telling anyone who would listen that he saw all but two of Aaron's home runs leading up to 715. This night in April, he was watching history unfold from the stadium press box.

Baseball entered a new era in 1976 when television mogul Ted Turner purchased the Atlanta Braves and promoted Davidson to vice president, but that situation didn't last long as Turner fired Donald because of a disagreement over a hotel suite Davidson had secured on a road trip.

Donald was confident he would get another job quickly and he did just that, acquiring employment in a matter of weeks with the Houston Astros as public relations director.

Donald Davidson died in 1990 at age 64 from throat cancer.

Ernie Johnson, from Brattleboro, Vermont, teamed up with Milo Hamilton to broadcast the Braves games on television and radio in 1974 as the Aaron drama unfolded. Johnson made a presentation to Aaron in pregame ceremonies.

Broadcaster Ernie Johnson honors Aaron. (Randy Cox)

The "Big E," as some called him, had an illustrious career in high school sports: all-state tight end in football, and basketball big man at center. He even played professional basketball for the American and Eastern leagues at the same time he was pitching minor league baseball. By 1952, it was baseball all the way for Ernie, as he pitched nine years for the Braves in the 1950s without a losing season. In 1974, he was named the Braves' associate director of broadcasting.

Johnson said one of his biggest thrills was pitching for the Milwaukee Braves in the 1957 World Series against the New York Yankees, appearing in three games and allowing only one run and two hits in seven innings. He added that another highlight of his broadcasting career was announcing three of Hank's big homers, his 500th, 600th, and 700th.

Ernie Johnson passed away on August 12, 2011, following a long illness.

GM Eddie Robinson presents a bronze bust to Henry. (Randy Cox)

With all those photographers and sports reporters jockeying for position to get close to the action on the field, it wasn't easy to chronicle everything that was happening. I remember when I got near Aaron as he was receiving his bronze bust during the pregame ceremony, I heard someone say, "quite a likeness," and it truly was.

Years later, Braves' public relations guru Bob Hope told me that he recalled his crew picking up the bust at the Atlanta Airport, and that it took a major effort to get it loaded into his station wagon and transported to Atlanta Stadium!

There was a record crowd that cool and rainy Monday night in April, and the ticket prices in 1974 were cool, too, at least by today's standards.

If you bought a children's General Admission ticket (12 & under), you would pay one dollar, while an adult could get a Gen Ad for two bucks. An upper level child seat was $1.50, while for adults it was $3.00; field level seats cost $4.50 for adults, $3.00 for kids. If you wanted to splurge and sit in the club or dugout level, it would have set you back a whopping $6.00.

A great likeness! (Randy Cox)

Eating at the stadium could be pretty costly as well, as recorded in the 1974 scorebook from that night: 50 cents for a regular hot dog, 55 cents for a kosher one; a quarter-pound hamburger, 65 cents; hot roast beef sandwich, $1.25; fish sandwich, 60 cents; French fries or slice of pizza, 35 cents; peanuts or popcorn served in a collectible megaphone, coffee or milk, 25 cents; ice cream or soft drinks, 30 cents; bottle beer, 65 to 75 cents; draft beer, 65 to 95 cents; and cigars, various prices.

In the 1970s, Joe McKellar oversaw the concession stands at Atlanta Stadium, and he estimated that about 200K of hamburgers were consumed by fans during a season, to go along with 150K of soft drinks, 300K bags of peanuts, and more than half a million hot dogs and sausages.

The pregame crowd is anxious for the action to start. (Randy Cox)

The Braves failed to crack the million-fan attendance mark in 1974…only 981,085 witnessed the team's third-place finish, in which they won a solid 88 games. It was the team's winningest season during the entire 13-year stretch between their first two division titles, in 1969 and 1982.

Football Legend and former head coach Bill Curry and his wife Carolyn were seated near Chief Noc-A-Homa's teepee in the left-field stands next to the foul pole. Nearby, journalist/author George Plimpton was observing the event for history and gathering material for his book on Aaron's 715th home run.

Curry's impression of the big night centered on Aaron's demeanor. "My biggest takeaway was that Aaron treated it as if it were business as usual," he said. "His dignity shone through. No celebration from him…true greatness."

Crowds Were Not Crowded

Not surprisingly, Atlanta stadium was sold out that night, a far cry from the tiny crowds near the end of the 1973 season, including: 2,872 when he hit his 710th on September 10 and 1,362 on September 17 when he smacked 711. Aaron's amazing pursuit in 1973 of the home run record did little to motivate fans, as the Braves drew only about 800,000 on the season. Manager Mathews said Atlanta was a good baseball town, it was just that the team needed to be a contender to draw big crowds. "...people have gotten away from us because we haven't won," he said.

Unfortunately for Carolyn, however, she selected the wrong time to visit the refreshment stand for a hot dog and soft drink, so she missed Aaron's record-breaking home run. "We all had fun with Carolyn and her hot dog delivery," Coach Curry said.

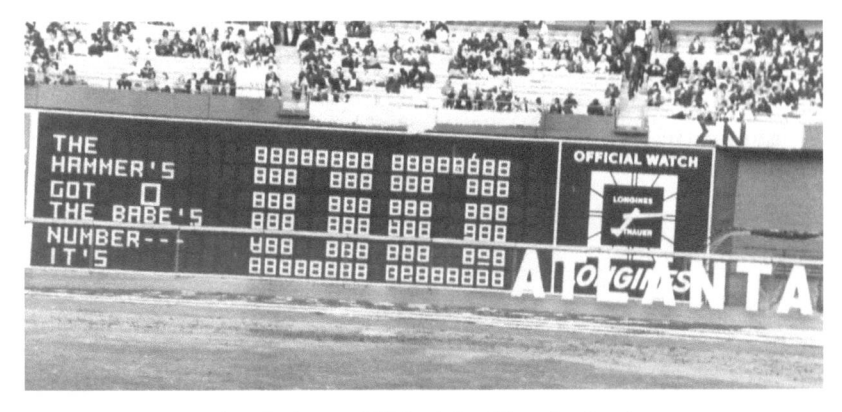

Jumbotron, 1974-style. (Randy Cox)

As part of the pregame ceremony, Noc-A-Homa entertained the capacity crowd with his Native American skills.

The Chief's real name was Levi Walker, Jr. and he was a full-blooded Native American (half Chipewa and half Ottowa) and a member of the Algonquin nation. Noc-A-Homa ran out onto the field, Braves players right behind him, and before he headed for his teepee he performed a "prayer dance" on the pitcher's mound. Clearly, that night the magic worked!

Chief Noc-A-Homa plays with fire, but in a good way. (Randy Cox)

During his time with the Braves, Walker made guest appearances in department stores for autograph sessions with children and adults alike.

Atlanta's Most Legendary Sports Mascot tells the whole story of the Chief's life. Noc-A-Homa became the Braves' mascot in 1966. Walker got the job starting in 1969, after convincing the Braves that the role should be performed by an actual Native American. Despite his heritage, the tolerance of historical stereotypes of Native Americans began to turn in the 1980s, and Atlanta retired the mascot after the 1985 season.

Chapter Five

Interview with Bob Hope, Former Braves' "Master of Public Relations"

In June 2023, while researching this book, I was thrilled to have a chance to speak first-hand with a gentleman who had been a friend of Henry Aaron for more than 55 years! Bob Hope, a career public relations professional, was with the Atlanta Braves for 14 years, including during the height of the Great Home Run Chase in the 1970s.

Hope began his college career at Georgia State University in Atlanta while working on the graveyard shift at Mead Packing Company making cardboard boxes. In 1965, he began his employment at Atlanta-Fulton County Stadium as an usher/errand boy when the Atlanta Crackers played their final season ahead of the Braves' move there.

"I made a list of a few places to work, and the Braves were at the top of the list," he said. "Anything would be better than the job that I had."

Lee Walburn, Braves' PR director at the time, set up an interview with Hope, asking him to write some sample press releases to apply for an entry level job. Hope provided some samples to Walburn, who declared them "pretty good," and he gave Hope the position in 1966.

"It was supposed to be a job for six months, but I just never left," Hope continued.

In 1967, he became PR director for the new Atlanta Chiefs soccer team and took over the Braves' PR reins in 1972 when Walburn resigned. He also did marketing and PR for the Ted Turner-owned Atlanta Hawks, despite warning Turner that he knew nothing about basketball! Hope left in 1979 to work for the Coca-Cola Company.

In 1994, he started a women's baseball team—the Colorado Silver Bullets—with seed money from Coors Beer. Phil Niekro was the manager.

"We had tryouts and test games for ladies, about 5,000 of them, who all wanted to play baseball," he said. The first year the team struggled to win, but by the fourth season the squad could compete with many men's teams.

"We think it provided the momentum for having women's sports teams in the U.S.," Hope said.

In 1991, Hope wrote a book titled, *We Could've Finished Last Without You: An Irreverent Look at the Atlanta Braves, the Losingest Team in Baseball for the Past 25 Years*. It is an interesting account of Bob's memories of working for the Braves where he originated numerous promotional events that have become legendary in the world of sports. He was even named "most innovative promoter" by *Sports Illustrated*.

In our interview, Hope talked to me about his role in the events leading up to Aaron's 714th and 715th home runs and their aftermath.

Hope's feelings on Aaron hitting home run 714 in Cincinnati, on April 4, 1974

Many issues swirled around Hank hitting his 714th home run in Cincinnati as the 1974 season began to get underway. The PR

Public relations guru Bob Hope poses with Aaron and Bob's grandson Henry—born on April 8, 2004, the 30th anniversary of Aaron's 715th home run. How's that for incredible timing?!
(Photo courtesy of Bob Hope)

man told me what was going on behind the scenes in Cincinnati and Atlanta. Of course, the powers that be in the Braves camp wanted Hank to tie AND break Ruth's record at home, and not necessarily very quickly, but Aaron's efficiency spoiled that.

Chairman of the Board Bartholomay, Traveling Secretary Donald Davidson, and other officials wanted to hold Henry out of all three games in Cincinnati, then have him resume his assault on the home run record in Atlanta during a long home stand (11 games) that started with the Dodgers on April 8.

"They wanted to just pull Aaron out of games in Cincinnati," Hope said. "I was very young then…and we made some decisions that weren't very smart."

He said he told management, "I don't think baseball is going to let you do that," just to keep him from hitting a home run because "Hank's going to do his best" to hit one.

"We could have had a long 11- or 12-game home stand to begin the season, but Donald suggested we could just hold Hank out from playing in Cincinnati," Hope said.

The whole situation, he said, could have been avoided in the initial scheduling process, as the Braves could have asked to start their season in Atlanta.

"It was incomprehensible that he would hit one on opening day on the road," but he did. "I was very concerned."

Hope was combatting ulcers worrying about the odds of Aaron smashing one on the road. "Obviously, despite our wishes, we couldn't hold him out."

"The crowd came to see Hank play. You can't be on national TV and hold him out," he said. "There weren't any threats. Kuhn just said you can't hold him out." The compromise was that Aaron would play in the first game, which was MLB's Opening Game of the 1974 season, sit out Game 2, and then be back in the lineup for the series finale.

Hope felt like Kuhn was villainized for nothing, because he (Kuhn) followed Hank's progress during the last two weeks of 1973. "He helped Hank along the way," he said.

"Bowie was a wonderful person – he came to Atlanta to help with fund raising for the Hank Aaron statue."

The media, as it tends to do, "just let it (holding out Hank) get blown out of proportion."

As for claims that Aaron didn't try his best in the third game in Cincy, Hope said, "Hank wasn't going to compromise doing his best under any circumstances. He was always going to try his best, even playing through death threats."

Another controversy cropped up at the last minute, as Aaron, at the suggestion of the Rev. Jesse Jackson, asked for a moment of silence during the first game in Cincy for the anniversary of the death of Martin Luther King, Jr., but the Reds said no.

Aaron received undue criticism for the Reds turning him down, but it was unfounded, Hope said. "The Braves had no control over what the Reds did," he said.

When Aaron failed to hit 715 in Cincinnati, the Braves' PR Department immediately turned their attention to the first game in Atlanta, having to gear up for "the greatest game in baseball history." Obviously, Hope wanted it to happen in Atlanta, eventually.

"Bowie Kuhn just made a bad call," Hope said (by not attending Atlanta's home opener). "Who would have thought Hank would hit two home runs in the first four games of the season?"

Getting ready for 715 and dealing with the media

Meanwhile, Hope and his staff turned to dealing with the legion of media from around the world coming to town to cover Henry Louis Aaron.

"The biggest thing for me was preparing for the media," he said. "We had 400 media people there. We had to close off the second level of the stadium where the club level seats were and set them up as press box seats."

Just giving out that many press passes was a tremendous task. In conjunction with the media throng, the Braves decided that photo position assignments would be first-come, first-served, regardless of who it was or what organization he or she represented.

A photographer covering the game called Hope, upset that a *Sports Illustrated* magazine photographer had pushed him aside from a prime position that he had occupied first.

"I held my ground and told the *SI* photographer you didn't get here early enough, so you will just have to find another spot," he said. "All the other photographers in the section broke into applause."

"Otherwise, everything seemed to go remarkably smooth," he said.

There was another decision the press and media corps didn't particularly like...the Braves clubhouse would be closed an hour, instead of a half-hour, before the game started, giving less access to Aaron and any other interview subjects.

Not just Aaron but the whole team needed to find time to go back into the clubhouse to relax before the game started.

Hope said that normally Hank was very cooperative with the media, going out of his way to help them. "Hank seemed to handle the pressure better than the rest of us did," he said.

In anticipating the number of media present, the PR Department set up a procedure to deal with their endless requests: interviews before the games and press conferences after.

"We gave the major media 15-minute segments for interviews with Hank," he said.

Adaptable artwork for Hank Aaron posters, artwork of the city, and the *Hank Aaron Sportscaster Guide* (sponsored by Magnavox), were made available to reporters. "I thought we did a nice job in supplying information to the media," he said.

Interview with Bob Hope

One time the Japanese media had more questions than Aaron had time for, so Bob conducted the interview through an interpreter.

"They questioned me as Hank, and five minutes into it, I thought I WAS Hank Aaron."

Hope shared a behind-the-scenes Aaron story that may surprise some readers. In July 1974, after Henry had hit #715, he had a rare display of displeasure with the media. In this case, it was the *Atlanta Journal* and the *Atlanta Constitution*. Several things appeared in the newspapers that Aaron didn't like: the running of a photo and cutline of wife Billye that Hank objected to; a story by *Journal* Braves beat writer Frank Hyland about Aaron's alleged double-talk concerning whether he wanted the Braves' managerial job; and a missing word in Sports Editor Jesse Outlar's column.

Not knowing Aaron's frame of mind, Hyland sauntered into the clubhouse before a game between the Braves and the San Diego Padres, where, after a lively discussion, Aaron abruptly threw a carton of strawberries, courtesy of Georgia Agriculture Day, into his face. When Frank arrived in the stadium press box, Bob joked that if his wife saw all that lipstick, he was going to be in trouble.

"That's not lipstick!" Hyland replied.

Although Henry may not have realized that Frank had nothing to do with the photo and caption or the Outlar typo, he was certainly right about Hyland writing the "double-talk" story. But Hyland paid a sticky price for all three incidents and for being in the wrong place at the wrong time.

"And I still kinda like the guy," Hyland said later.

In an article about the strawberry incident written in the *Atlanta Constitution*, reporter Charlie Roberts said Aaron made the only hit at the Stadium Friday night as the Padres' game was rained out. "And they didn't even play a game," he wrote.

Hope on 715th evening and aftermath

As for preparing for the home opener in Atlanta, the top management from Bartholomay on down was very cooperative, according to Bob Hope.

"Bill Bartholomay was great," he said. "Vice President Dick Cecil ran the business side of the operation."

"We had the whole off-season (1973-74) to figure out what we wanted to do," he said.

The biggest challenge the staff faced concerned selling tickets that weren't computerized like they are today – printing about 12,000 to 50,000 tickets in 24 hours.

"Back then we had to have a hard ticket for every seat. Just the ability to sell that many tickets that fast was a challenge," he said.

"I think if we had gotten through the second night, I think people would have started buying tickets in advance," he added.

There was a Japanese company that wanted to construct a bronze bust of Hank using advanced technology, taking laser measurements around his head. When it was finished, the PR team had to retrieve it from the Atlanta Airport.

"I don't think we had any idea how heavy that bust was!" Hope said. "We put it into the back seat of my Toyota...and kind of rolled it out of the car at the stadium."

Other pregame preparations included painting center field with an American flag on a U.S. map for a special ceremony, "This Is Your Life, Hank Aaron." Family members, celebrities, and baseball officials took part.

Interview with Bob Hope

A lot of excitement was happening. "We lined up choirs to sing, and fireworks would go off. 715 was the greatest moment in the history of baseball."

"Before the game, the atmosphere was electric because you knew you might see something that night that would be historic," Hope said.

After the game was over, he felt like it was a "combination of disbelief and frustration. I was really hoping it would go several more days."

Hope and staff oversaw getting everything set up downstairs in a football locker room for the post-game press conference, making sure everything would run smoothly because he knew it was going to be a "mob scene."

"Mathews wanted 10 minutes to talk to the players" before the media was allowed in.

As several hundred photographers and reporters crammed into the room, Hank and Billye were up front sitting at a table with a 715 logo in the background. I was there, taking photographs of the pair, listening as Henry reacted with poise, dignity, and modesty answering the questions from the world's media.

The lady streaker and Atlanta Boys Choir

Hope recounted some other "excitement" that occurred around the time of Hank's 715th home run, some unexpected commotion in the left-field stands.

"There was a streaker in the upper deck…she was the most ignored streaker in the history of streaking. She was a pretty girl, and was wearing a raincoat," Hope said.

"She took off her raincoat, had nothing on underneath, and ran down the aisle butt-naked, and sat in some guy's lap."

Hope said she leaped up, put on the raincoat, and left. Hope told the ushers, "Just ignore her, nobody really saw her" other than the guy whose lap she sat in.

"She just picked the wrong time to streak!" he concluded. Apparently, there is no photographic evidence of this event.

The Atlanta Boys Choir was scheduled to sing during the pregame ceremony, but couldn't make it, so a coed choir was substituted for them.

"It was erroneously reported in the local media the next morning that the Atlanta Boys Choir had appeared, and that they also have girls," Hope said.

Security problems and a dangerous situation

One incident was recorded and has been viewed millions of times in the replay of home run #715. This is, of course, the two infamous young men who ran onto the field and joined Aaron for part of his trip around the bases.

"They were lucky that they didn't get shot," Hope said. "Calvin (Wardlaw, Henry's bodyguard) was really the last line of defense."

Security measures around the stadium and on the field were not like they are today. "Security worked to keep people away from the celebrities sitting in the stands and boxes. We didn't even think about guys jumping on the field from the stands."

Hope disagreed with the media report that 20,000 fans left after the home run. "That was an exaggeration," he said. "People stayed for the game. If they did leave, they left in the eighth inning [after Aaron had come out of the game]."

Hate mail

As reported by the press, Hank did receive a ton of mail, but only a small percentage was hate mail, according to Hope.

"He didn't get bags of hate mail...the media exaggerated."

"The masses of people (writing letters) were very supportive," he said. "...most of the fans idolized Hank."

"The people who sent hate mail were just bitter and racist and very dangerous."

Working with his buddy

"Over the years I became one of Hank's close friends," Hope recalled. "Dusty Baker and I were the only two non-family pallbearers at his funeral." There were about 100 honorary pallbearers.

Henry Aaron was a champion of civil rights and spoke out for minority causes. His career and life had an immeasurable impact on civil rights in America.

Bob Hope enjoyed working with the slugger on events, such as Aaron's 62nd birthday party. Hank was set to coordinate it but asked Hope to do it as the Home Run King was going to be roasted.

Hope said Aaron's advisors sometimes could be cranky and cause you problems, but with Henry himself, that was never the case. "He was always gentlemanly."

The two remained close friends until Hank passed away in 2021. "He called me a month before he died and wanted me to come see him," Hope said. "I told him that I did not want to be the one to give Hank Aaron COVID-19." Aaron had just had his first COVID shot.

"I never thought about Hank Aaron needing a friend. I had been his friend for so many years and I was one person who never went to him and tried to abuse the relationship in any way."

Hope said he would go out and sit with Hank. One time Aaron had just read a book about the late supreme court justice Thurgood Marshall, and he wanted to talk about it or the movie "42" about Jackie Robinson's life.

"There was no bitterness in Hank, and I don't think he would have liked to come across to people as a bitter man."

The highlight of his career, Hope said, was "the relationship with Hank Aaron over the years." How could it not have been?

Chapter Six

Henry Aaron and Me

While I studied journalism in college during the late 1960s and early 70s, it was hard for me to make time to attend Braves games and see Aaron work his magic at the "Launching Pad," as I also worked 30 hours in the Circulation and Advertising Departments for the *Atlanta Journal*.

Since I lived in Decatur, an easy driving distance of the stadium, I was able to keep up with the team pretty well. One thing is for sure: it was rare for there to be a shortage of tickets.

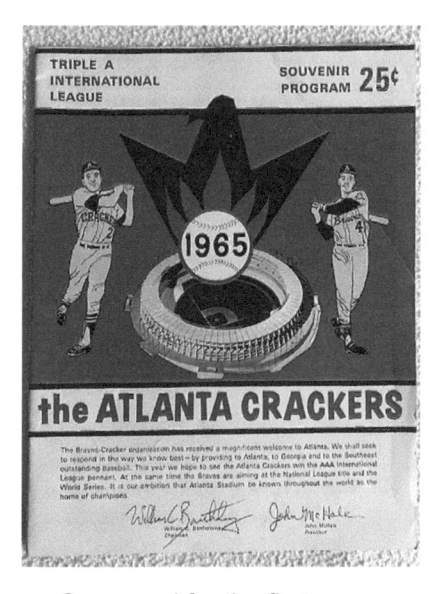

Scorecard for the first game played in Atlanta Stadium involving major league teams, an exhibition game between the Braves and Tigers, April 9, 1965. (Author's Collection)

Before the night of the 715th homer, I had been blessed with experiencing several other special Henry Aaron moments at the ballpark: My dad and I attended the first exhibition game played at Atlanta Stadium in 1965, between the Braves and the Detroit Tigers. We were at the first game of the 1969 National

League Championship Series against the New York Mets. And I was in the ballpark in 1971 for Aaron's 600th home run, against San Francisco – quite a stroke of luck for the first assignment of my journalism career!

My family, friends, and I had some great times watching the Atlanta Crackers at Ponce de Leon Ballpark from 1958 through 1964, and when the Braves moved to Atlanta in 1966, it was a dream come true to see Aaron, Mathews, and all those great players we had only witnessed before on small black-and-white television sets and on baseball cards, some of which ended up on my bicycle spokes, for heaven's sakes! The players pictured on those cards were now flesh and blood, and they were playing in our town and in our state!

In the first baseball game involving major league teams played in the Southeast, the Braves defeated the Tigers, 6-3, on April 9, 1965, before 37,232 fans, in the first of three weekend exhibition contests. We were disappointed that Henry Aaron couldn't play in the game because of a recent ankle injury, but rejoiced as brother Tommie upheld the family tradition by launching the first home run ever hit in Atlanta Stadium and receiving a standing ovation to boot! What a game! The Braves took the entire series and were ready to start the 1965 season in Cincinnati with home games set for County

Gary Gentry was a flame-thrower in his early years with the Mets, but arm troubles plagued him after the Braves obtained him in 1973. (Public Domain)

Stadium in Milwaukee, against the Cubs. Due to the injury, Aaron did not start a game until the Braves' ninth contest of the season.

1969 National League Championship Series

In 1969, the same year Aaron was named team captain, Gary Gentry was a pitcher for the New York Mets and took the mound on his 23rd birthday for Game Three of the first-ever National League Championship Series against the Braves at Atlanta Stadium. That year, MLB had undergone expansion and two NL and AL division winners played each other for the chance to battle it out in the World Series.

Gentry was hit hard, including surrendering Aaron's third home run of the three-game series, and was relieved in the third, but was bailed out by a young Nolan Ryan as the Mets roared back to sweep the series and advance to the Fall Classic against the Orioles. No blame for the Braves' failure could be assigned to Aaron, who homered in each game, had two doubles, drove in seven runs, and even gunned down a runner at third in the final game.

My dad and I were fortunate enough to see Game 1 in the new format, though it was hard to watch the Mets push across five runs in the eighth inning to seal the win after Aaron had given the Braves a brief lead with a tie-breaking homer in the bottom of the seventh. We sat in the right-field stands (Upper

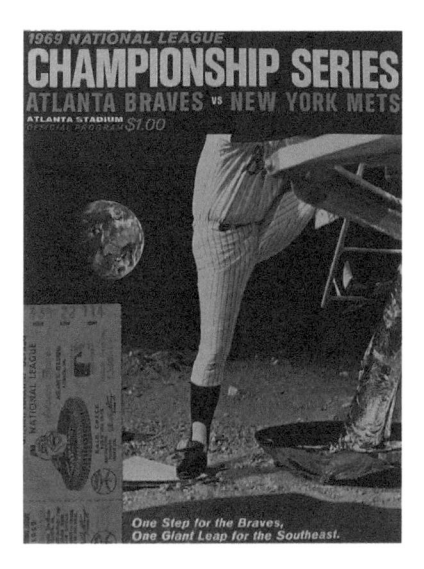

Ticket stub and official game program for the 1969 NLCS Game 1, October 4, 1969. (Author's Collection)

Pavilion, $3.00, tax included), watching ace Tom Seaver overcome a double and home run by Aaron to pitch the Mets to a 9-5 victory.

Gentry was traded to the Braves in the off-season of 1972 and was on the field to congratulate Aaron after he hit #715.

Hank got a measure of revenge four years later, Sunday, July 8, 1973, when he was welcomed to Shea Stadium in New York, deep into his home run chase. It turned out to be an unofficial Hank Aaron Day, as The Hammer clouted two home runs off former Braves pitcher George Stone (his 22nd and 23rd of the season) to hurtle Atlanta to a 4-2 victory over the Mets. His second homer was the 696th of his career.

It was quite a day for a visiting player to experience, as Aaron received six standing ovations in all, the first coming during batting practice! Aaron remarked at the time that the Big Apple was "one of his favorite cities," and it's no wonder why.

Aaron's success against the Mets and the rest of the National League was a credit to his excellence, not due to any favors done for him, such as pitchers "grooving" them for the slugger. A month earlier, in June, Commissioner Kuhn read pitchers' comments in an Associated Press story that they were going to give Aaron pitches right down the middle. Kuhn reacted (or overreacted) by sending a letter to National League clubs, stating, "…any such conduct would violate the requirements of major league Rule 21 that every player must give his best efforts toward the winning of any baseball game in which he is involved." Violators will be suspended, the letter stated. Pitchers certainly knew, as Kuhn should have, that Henry Aaron needed no help from them to get more than his share of home runs.

600th Home Run

A lasting Henry Louis Aaron memory of mine occurred on Tuesday, April 27, 1971, when he smacked his 600th career home run off San

Henry Aaron and Me

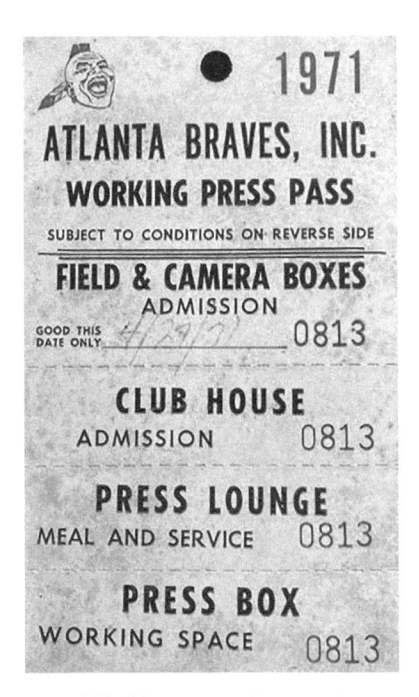

Working press box and photographer's credentials for the game of April 27, 1971, Atlanta Braves versus San Francisco Giants, in which Henry Aaron hit his 600th home run. (Author's Collection)

Francisco pitcher and Hall of Famer Gaylord Perry. As a journalism student at Georgia State University about four miles from Atlanta Stadium, I was lucky enough to be in the press box that night, covering the game for the *GSU Signal* campus newspaper, alongside Braves' beat reporters Hal Hayes and Wayne Minshew of *The Atlanta Constitution*. Those reporters were two of my journalistic favorites, and helped fuel my desire to continue reporting, especially in the world of sports. I hardly knew at the time that in three short years I would be back again for the sports story of the century!

In my by-lined story, published in the May 6, 1971 edition, Henry commented on home run number 600, stating that he "felt like it was going" as soon as he hit it. Perry, he commented, was always a tough competitor, and had tried to jam him on an inside pitch. Aaron crunched the two-run homer in the third inning near Chief Noc-A-Homa's teepee in left field. Aaron and Perry were frequent foes over the years, and overall Gaylord held his own. In 109 career at-bats against Perry, Aaron batted .294 but went deep only three times and struck out 20.

The only downside for Braves fans was the outcome of the game, as the Giants, behind Willie Mays' tenth-inning RBI heroics, won 6-5.

Post-game, a photographer came around with a picture of Aaron and his home run swing. Asked to analyze the blast, Aaron smiled and simply said, "There it goes."

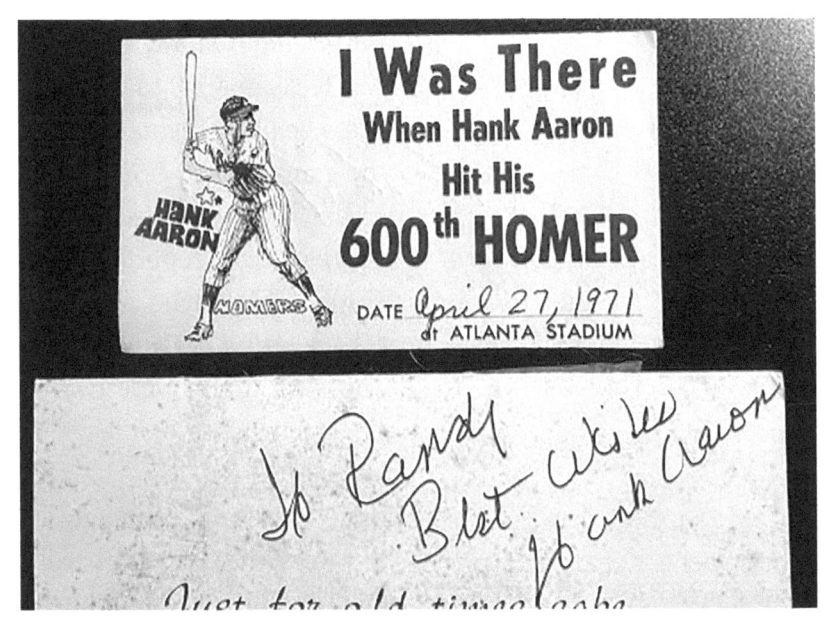

"I Was There…600th Homer" card and my hero's autograph, personalized to me, a cherished possession. (Author's Collection)

Hank came close to hitting one out in the first inning, but it landed for a double in right field. "I didn't think that one was going out," he said.

Talking to the news media after the game, he was asked whether he thought he had a chance to break Babe Ruth's HR record of 714 homers. "That's a long way off," he said. "I'll just try to get one home run at a time."

Aaron said that he would like to be thought of as a good all-around hitter, not just one who hit home runs, stating that his 3,000th hit the previous season was a bigger thrill than his 600th HR. "The greatest thrill of all" will be hitting his 700th home run, he concluded.

715 HR Collectibles

Hank Aaron memorabilia has always sold well through the years and should continue to do well in the future, as fan interest in The Hammer continues to grow. Game programs, ticket stubs, photographs, telegrams received by Aaron, anniversary patches, bobbleheads, baseball gloves, bats, and baseballs are just some of the items that Aaron collectors collect.

In the bygone days of the 60s and 70s, it was quite possible to get players to sign autographs for free! I was lucky enough to get signatures from Brooks Robinson, Phil Niekro, Dale Murphy, Mickey Mantle...and Hank Aaron – twice! The first one Henry signed for me was following his 600th home run night; the other he gave to me through a work colleague, Jackie McKenzie, who happened to see him at a greeting card shop one day at lunch. I will always treasure those autographs.

And let's not forget about baseball cards. At the end of the 1973 season, the Topps Company faced a decision to produce a large amount (some say 2 million) of Aaron cards for 1974 (two months before the season started), proclaiming him the Home Run King although at that point he was two round-trippers shy. The risk was taken, and Aaron didn't disappoint. His 1974 card (Number 1) was printed in a horizontal format and can sell on eBay for $35 to $100, depending on condition.

Another example of a fine collectible is the game program for the "Night of 715." It features on the cover Aaron and Donald Davidson, the Braves' traveling secretary and his good friend since their time together in Milwaukee. Prices range from about $25 to $100.

There was a huge contingent of photographers on the record-breaking night, but most of the photos were focused on the 715th home run, making for a lack of variety.

Atlanta-Fulton County Stadium

Foul lines in left and right field were 330 feet, and 402 feet in center, with six-foot wire fences. Builders were Thompson and Street of Charlotte, North Carolina, and Atlanta. Project architects were Heery & Heery and Finch; Alexander, Barnes, Rothschild & Paschal, both of Atlanta. Seating capacity was 52,500 in 1965, 52,013 in 1992.

When Roberto Clemente of the Pittsburgh Pirates first saw Atlanta Stadium in April 1966, he commented that it was "beautiful." "I like it...very much," he said. This stadium, he said, would no doubt benefit the hometown Braves because of their "great power" to hit home runs.

Clyde King, the Bucs' pitching coach at the time and future Braves' manager, said neither wind nor background would be a factor here. "...the distances are fair to both hitters and pitchers," he said.

The last game played there was on Oct. 24, 1996.

Demolition

At 8:04 AM on August 2, 1997, the stadium was demolished in only 27 seconds, using 1,600 pounds of carefully placed explosives. Ten thousand tons of structural steel and 35,000 cubic yards of concrete turned into a jumbled mess as a shroud of dust blossomed in the Atlanta sky. Demolition Dynamics, Inc. of Franklin, Tennessee was in charge, a spokesman saying everything went off "perfectly, just as we expected."

I managed to stand near the folks whose company did all the work to make sure the explosion came off as planned. It was sad that the house where Aaron and the Braves, the Atlanta Falcons, and Atlanta Chiefs soccer team had performed so many wonderful feats was now history. One consolation: a part of the left-center field wall where the 715th home run went over was preserved as a monument to Aaron.

Built in 11 months, Atlanta Fulton-County Stadium was demolished in minutes. (Randy Cox)

An Atlanta crowd of an estimated 30,000 showed up to watch outside of an 800-foot buffer zone. Workers came in later to pave the 14 acres as a parking lot for the then-new Turner Field, used during the 1996 Atlanta Summer Olympic Games, but taken over by the Braves as their new home following the Olympiad. "It really...heralded our entry into major league sports, the first southern city to have a pro sports franchise," said then mayor Bill Campbell of the old facility. After the dust cleared, seats from the stadium went on sale for $100 each, one of which I purchased myself.

The future holds promising things for the area: property owner Georgia State University is scheduled to soon start construction of a state-of-the-art baseball park for its collegiate athletes. Officials have said Henry Aaron's wall will be part of the facility.

Henry takes time out to sign autographs during Spring Training, circa 1970. (Marion Johnson photographs, VIS 33.80.41, Kenan Research Center at Atlanta History Center)

Chapter Seven
Play Ball! The Game's Supporting Cast

Official program for "The Game," April 8, 1974, with Henry and Donald Davidson on the cover. (Author's Collection)

Eddie Mathews, the volatile Braves skipper and long-time teammate of Henry Aaron, was one of the first to greet The Hammer following his entrance onto the big stage. The former slugger had started his second full managerial season in 1974, having had his uniform number (41) retired in 1969. He played on two Atlanta teams, the Braves and the Southern League Crackers. As a Cracker in 1950, Mathews clobbered 32 homers, the first 30-homer season for the franchise since Les Burge in 1941.

Batgirls clean up around home plate as Braves' catcher Vic Correll patiently awaits the start of the game. (Randy Cox)

Mathews was selected for 10 National League All-Star teams and spearheaded the Milwaukee Braves to victory in the 1957 World Series against the New York Yankees with his hitting (home run in the seventh game) and fielding (making the final out at third base). He was a star at a very young age, belting 47 home runs in his second season at age 21, which he followed with two more consecutive 40-homer years. Mathews is considered one of the best third basemen in the history of baseball.

As "dynamic duo" teammates in the 1950s and 60s, Mathews and Aaron blasted more circuit blows combined than Babe Ruth/Lou Gehrig or Mickey Mantle/Roger Maris with the Yankees. When new General Manager Paul Richards traded Mathews to the Houston Astros in 1966, his fans, including myself, and Aaron were infuriated. Mathews did have the good fortune to wrap up his career in 1968 as a backup on the World Series winning Detroit Tigers.

"T-Bone"

The late Tommie Aaron (aka T-Bone) was close to his older brother Henry, though realistic about their relative prowess on the field. They were two different types of ballplayers, Tommie said. He had to work very hard to make it in baseball, while his famous brother was a "complete ballplayer... who could do just about anything."

In June 1973, T-Bone was named by Braves' GM Eddie Robinson the new manager of the Southern League's Savannah team (Double-A). At the time, Tommie had 15 years of experience in pro ball as a player, six with the Braves, having started with the Eau Claire, Wisconsin team in 1958, the same club his elder brother had played for.

Tommie Aaron had four 20-plus home run seasons in the minors, but never hit more than eight in a season in the majors. (Marion Johnson photographs, VIS 33.069.002, Kenan Research Center at Atlanta History Center)

> The first Black manager of an organized team in the South, Tommie was quite proud that he and Hank produced more home runs together than any other brothers in MLB history: 755 for Hank, 13 for Tommie, for a total of 768.
>
> Tommie was unable to be with Henry on his record-breaking night because he was managing the Savannah Braves. Later, he managed the Richmond Braves of the International League.
>
> Tommie died of leukemia on August 16, 1984. He was only 45.

Mathews played for the Braves in all three hometown cities: Boston, Milwaukee and Atlanta, a feat no other player can claim. The great third baseman also was featured on the cover of the inaugural issue of a new magazine, *Sports Illustrated*, on August 16, 1954.

Mathews was fired midseason in 1974 and was succeeded by Clyde King. I was particularly upset because Eddie had been an inspiration to me since third base was my position in Little League, and I tried to emulate his feats on the diamond.

The Braves' Opening Night lineup looked like this:

Ralph Garr, RF

Mike Lum, 1B

Darrell Evans, 3B

Henry Aaron, LF

Dusty Baker, CF

Davey Johnson, 2B

Vic Correll, C

Craig Robinson, SS

Ron Reed, P

As the pregame festivities unfolded, several Atlanta players were on the field next to the batgirls, including Buzz Capra, Paul Casanova, Vic Correll, Norm Miller, and Leo Foster.

Casanova was considered a very good defensive catcher throughout his eight-year career, which included catching Phil Niekro's no-hitter on August 5, 1973.

Correll's most productive season came in 1975, when as a Brave he posted career numbers in home runs (11), RBI (39) and games played (103).

Miller scored the winning run in a 24-inning game in 1968 when the Astros bested the New York Mets on Bob Aspromonte's bases-loaded ground ball that went through the legs of Mets' shortstop Al Weis for an error.

Shortstop Foster seemed to be snake-bit in his MLB debut, when he broke in with the Braves on July 9, 1971, at Three Rivers Stadium in Pittsburgh. He committed an error on the first ball hit to him. And at the plate, he hit into a double play in the fifth inning and a triple play in the seventh.

The Braves had several outstanding players on the 1974 team. In addition to Aaron breaking the Babe's home run record, Ralph Garr won the National League batting title with a .353 average, Buzz Capra garnered the ERA title (2.28) and pitcher Phil Niekro tied for the NL lead in wins with 20.

Darrell Evans had a memorable 21-year career, compiling 414 home runs, four seasons with 30 home runs or more, 8,973 at-bats, a .248 batting average, 1,354 runs batted in, capping

Ralph Garr swings away in the first inning. (Randy Cox)

it off with a World Series championship with the 1984 Detroit Tigers. Evans led the AL in home runs with 40 at age 38 and collected more than 1600 bases on balls in his career, about 200 more than he struck out. He retired in 1990 at age 42.

Aaron made a special point in mentoring his younger teammate, Ralph "Road Runner" Garr, who set an Atlanta Braves team record in 1973 for stolen bases (35). He began the 1974 season with the highest batting average of any active player in the major leagues (.318) and was later voted a National League All-Star.

"Whatever God gave you, that's what will keep you here," Aaron advised his protégé. "So, whatever you did in the minor leagues to get here, that's what you do when you're here...".

Batting ahead of Aaron, Davey Johnson, Dusty Baker, and Darrell Evans, the speedy Garr was an excellent table setter. He could have stolen more bases, but why bother with that powerhouse lineup hitting after him? "God blessed me with good speed..." he said.

Dusty Baker on Deck

Dusty Baker watched home run #715 from the on deck circle. Baker not only had an excellent career as a player, but enjoyed spectacular success as a manager as well. In his 19-year playing career (1968-86) with the Braves, Dodgers, Giants, and Athletics, he hit 242 home runs and drove in 1,013. He spent 26 years as a manager for the Giants, Cubs, Reds, Nationals, and Astros, retiring at the end of the 2023 season with a career record of 2183-1862 (.540).

Dusty Baker has said that no one had a greater impact on his development as a ballplayer and leader than Henry Aaron. (Marion Johnson photographs, VIS 33.78.72, Kenan Research Center at Atlanta History Center)

Baker lost the 2021 World Series to the Braves, but his Astros came back the following year to defeat the Phillies, making him the oldest manager to win a title. Other achievements include being the 12th overall and first African-American manager with 2,000 victories; 13 postseason appearances in 26 years as a manager, including the last eight years of his career; ninth manager to win both NL and AL pennants; and first manager in MLB history to lead five different teams to division titles.

Garr was traded from the Braves to the White Sox after the 1975 season. He hit exactly .300 in his first two years in the AL and retired in 1980 after a handful of games with the California Angels, saying he had put baseball out of his system. Garr's career batting average is an impressive .306, one point higher than Aaron's, though Aaron outhomered The Road Runner by 680.

Aaron's first at-bat, leading off the second, produced a different kind of record against Dodgers' pitcher Al Downing. After Aaron drew a walk, Dusty Baker knocked home Henry with a double, and as Henry touched the plate, he broke Willie Mays' NL record for runs scored. Mays had once told Aaron this was a great record because that was the name of the game: to score runs!

Nicknames were plentiful for Aaron, including "Bad Henry," (Aaron's favorite, given to him by ace Los Angeles Dodgers' pitchers Sandy Koufax and Don Drysdale), "Mr. Wrists," "Supes (Superstar)," and "The Hammer." "Hammerin' Hank" was suggested by assistant to the chairman Donald Davidson.

"Say-Hey Kid"

Some baseball aficionados said that Henry Aaron and Willie Mays were too competitive to be friends, but that statement was refuted by The Hammer and his mother, Mrs. Estella Aaron, who said Willie "was one of Hank's best friends in baseball...none closer than Willie." The "Say-Hey Kid" had similar roots to Aaron's, hailing from Fairfield, Alabama, a suburb of Birmingham. As of this writing, Mays, at 92, is the oldest living member of the Baseball Hall of Fame.

Three years Henry's senior, Willie finished his incredible career with 660 home runs, 12 Gold Gloves, appearances in 24 All-Star games, two MVPs, and a World Series championship with the New York Giants in 1954 when he made the spectacular over-the-shoulder catch of Vic Wertz's drive with his back to home plate. He was elected to the Hall of Fame in 1970.

Willie and Henry both loved the game of baseball. Before his manager Leo Durocher put a stop to it, Mays would join up with a bunch of kids after a game at the Polo Grounds and play stickball with them in the streets.

"All I know is that Mays' presence makes my job a lot easier," said Durocher after Willie's arrival in 1951, stating that the charismatic center fielder was solely responsible for the "life and spirit" the team didn't have the previous year.

Willie Mays, who some people consider the best all-around baseball player in MLB history, served two years in the U.S. Army (1952-53), playing 180 games for the Fort Eustis Wheels. Had he not missed those two seasons, it is likely Mays would have surpassed 700 home runs during his career and may have challenged Ruth's record, too.

During the winter of 1955, Mays organized a barnstorming team consisting of all Black players which Aaron said was "possibly the best team ever assembled": Monte Irvin, Lary Doby, Mays and Aaron in the outfield; Ernie Banks at shortstop; Roy Campanella, catcher; George Crowe, Harry Thompson, and Junior Gilliam in the infield; and pitchers Don Newcombe, Joe Black, Sam Jones, and Brooks Lawrence.

> ### *Running the Bases Backwards?*
>
> After The Hammer had tied the record at 714, he began thinking about what might happen when he clubbed #715. Said Aaron to a reporter: "Well, I only need one

> more now. When I hit that next one, I'll probably run around the bases backwards." Back in 1969, Aaron had given the same advice to Chicago Cubs' Ernie Banks ahead of the great infielder's 500th homer. "Why don't you do like Jim Piersall did when he hit a homer – run the bases backwards?" Hank suggested. Piersall did run the bases in the correct order – but backwards – after he hit his 100th home run on June 23, 1963.

Davey Johnson, known more for his defensive play than his offense, blasted 43 homers for the Braves in 1973 to lead the team, three more than Aaron had. In so doing, he shattered the 51-year-old HR record for second basemen set by Rogers Hornsby. With three Gold Gloves under his belt at Baltimore, Johnson had never surpassed 18 homers in one season.

Johnson credited his success to batting behind Aaron and third baseman Darrell Evans, who joined the 40-homer club with 41 and to the air at the "Launching Pad." "…a pitcher can bear down just so long," Johnson said. "Maybe he was losing a little concentration by the time he got to me."

Just talking to Henry Aaron helped him at the plate, Johnson said. He (Johnson) became "more aggressive…The feeling around here…is that we are up there to attack the baseball, and having that feeling is half the battle."

Johnson finished his 13-year career with 136 home runs, 609 RBIs, 564 runs scored, 1,252 hits, and played in four All-Star games. He retired in 1978 after playing for the Baltimore Orioles, the Braves, Philadelphia Phillies, and Chicago Cubs.

Davey Johnson takes a cut. Johnson and Baker combined for more than 3,500 wins in their managerial careers. (Randy Cox)

As a manager, Johnson's career win-loss record in 17 seasons was 1,372-1,071, with the Dodgers Orioles, Mets, Reds, and Nationals, for an outstanding overall winning percentage of .562. With the Mets, he won the 1986 World Series, and was awarded AL Manager of the Year in 1997 after leading the Orioles to 98 wins and NL Manager of the Year in 2012 when his Washington Nationals took the NL East crown.

Babe Ruth

Whether you called him "Bambino," the "Sultan of Swat," "Big Fella," or just "Babe," everyone knew who you were talking about. On May 25, 1935, the Boston Braves' newly acquired aging slugger hit three homers in one game against the Pittsburgh Pirates to bring his career total to 714, a record no one thought would ever be broken. The last went completely out of cavernous Forbes Field, the first player ever to do that. Like Aaron, Ruth was 40 years old when he hit home run #714, and interestingly, their birthdays are one day apart, Aaron on February 5th and Ruth on February 6th.

According to Yankee teammate Earle Combs, the Babe would usually hit with a 42-ounce bat, but sometimes he would grab a whopping 50-ounce piece of lumber, naming his bats "Big Bertha," "Black Betsy," and "Beautiful Bella."

Ruth began his baseball career as a left-handed catcher for St. Mary's Industrial School for Boys in Maryland, but quickly switched to pitching. A Baltimore Orioles scout observed his play, offering him a contract for $600 a month to play for the club's International League team.

Not long after that, the Boston Red Sox bought the 19-year-old's contract for $3,000 and gave him a salary of $2,500 a year. Ruth went 2-1 in four appearances as a 19-year-old, and then blossomed into one of the top pitchers in the American League, winning 18, 23, and 24 games the next three seasons, picking up an ERA title in 1916 and throwing a 14-inning complete game (allowing only 6 hits) in that season's Fall Classic. By 1918, Babe the slugger began to overtake Babe the pitcher, as Ruth won 13 of 20 games he pitched in, but also hit 11 home runs to lead the league in that category. By comparison, Aaron was 20 when the Milwaukee Braves brought him up to the majors as an outfielder. And although The Hammer played some second base in the early years of his career, he never pitched in a big league game.

Babe Ruth, batting in an exhibition game at Ponce de Leon Park in Atlanta. (Bill Wilson photographs, VIS 99.449.01, Kenan Research Center at Atlanta History Center)

After the 1919 season, Ruth was infamously sold to the New York Yankees for $125,000 and a $300,000 loan (with Fenway Park as collateral), which more than 100 years later remains the Red Sox's stadium. The Bambino smacked a previously unimaginable 54 home runs in 1920 as the Yankees doubled their previous season's attendance at nearly 1.3 million. In 1923, the Yankees left the Polo Grounds and into "The House that Ruth Built."

In 1927, Ruth broke his own single-season home run record when he blasted 60, a mark that stood until Roger Maris of the Yankees clobbered 61 in 1961.

Like Aaron with the Milwaukee Brewers, Ruth ended his career where he began, in Boston, ironically also with the Braves. The Babe's skills had greatly faded by the time he went to the Braves, and was suggested that he was hired to be "vice president in charge of keeping the Boston Braves from starving to death" during the Great Depression.

Ruth retired on June 2, 1935, and passed away from esophageal cancer on August 16, 1948, in New York.

Paul Gallico, an author and sportswriter during Ruth's era, described his voice as "deep and hoarse, his speech crude and earthy. He had an eye that was abnormally quick, nerves and muscular reactions to match, supple wrists, a murderous swing, and a gorgeously truculent, competitive spirit."

Ruth and Aaron were two very different types of men and led very different lifestyles. Ruth was very loud, impulsive, and outgoing, while Aaron was more of a private person. However, they did have a lot of things in common, according to Charlie Grimm, manager of the Milwaukee Braves when Aaron was elevated to the team in 1954.

Both players had complete looseness and relaxation while at the plate, he said. "Both knew the strike zone and swung the bat...".

Pitchers had trouble finding any weak points to exploit with either player, Grimm said. In addition, Hank and the Babe both had an excellent sense of humor, were extremely generous with their time and friendly towards fans, and both had a good rapport with children.

Babe Ruth received no additional attention when he set baseball's career home run record. In fact, it's unlikely anyone was aware at the time who the previous record-holder was, 19th-century slugger Roger Connor of the New York Giants, who retired after the 1897 season with 138 home runs. Connor was one of the best hitters of baseball's earliest era, finishing his career with more than 2,400 hits, 800 extra-base hits, and a batting average of .316.

Connor was elected to baseball's Hall of Fame in 1976, an accomplishment for which Henry Aaron deserves indirect credit. As Aaron approached Ruth's record, the baseball world began to wonder whose record Ruth had broken, which shone the spotlight on Connor and his excellent career. Connor passed away in 1931, several years before the Hall came into existence.

In another piece of numerical magic, the pitcher Aaron would face was also #44, the veteran left-hander, Al Downing. After breaking in with the Yankees in 1961, Downing had led the AL in strikeouts in 1964. As a Dodger in 1973, he had given up two homers (676 and 693) to The Hammer, but still came away with a victory in both games.

Number 44 prepares for his first at-bat—10 feet in front of the first-base photographers' box! (Randy Cox)

As for his number 44, Aaron said that when he came to his first Spring Training with the Braves he wanted a low number, because for some reason most players with high numbers didn't seem to stick around too long. He wore number 5 as a rookie, but then, saying he wanted a double number, landed on 44 from his second season on. That Downing also wore 44 for the Dodgers only adds to the mystique. Aaron, who hit 44 homers in four seasons of his career, saw his number retired in 1977.

Just another at-bat for The Hammer. (Randy Cox)

Prior to the start of the 1971 season, the Milwaukee Brewers traded Downing to the Los Angeles Dodgers for Andy Kosco. To say it was a lopsided trade for the Dodgers would be an understatement. In his first season in the National League, Downing won 20 games and hurled a league-leading five shutouts. He earned NL Comeback Player of the Year honors as well as finishing third in NL Cy Young Award balloting behind winner Ferguson Jenkins and Tom Seaver.

"I was proud to be out on the mound at that moment," Al Downing said. "Those are things you don't anticipate when you begin your career; you just anticipate having a good career. This was a record that many people thought, because of the myth of Babe Ruth, would never be broken. So much of it was based on longevity and productivity over a long period of time."

"Naturally, I wished I could have won the ball game, but you can't have everything."

Play Ball! The Game's Supporting Cast

Move over Bambino.... (Randy Cox)

Two lucky fans pose with Henry in the press box of Atlanta Stadium, which was still under construction. (Marion Johnson photographs, VIS 33.68.11, Kenan Research Center at Atlanta History Center)

Chapter Eight
Exclusive Interviews: Ron Reed & Buzz Capra

Ron Reed fires a strike as "The Game" gets underway! (Randy Cox)

Ron Reed

Pitcher Ron "Slinky" Reed, a 6'6", 230-pound right-hander, started the game for the hometown Braves, before being pinch hit for during the Braves' two-run rally in the sixth. Reed was relieved by Buzz Capra, who threw three shutout innings to preserve the win for Reed. Before becoming a major league pitcher, Reed played hoops for two seasons with the Detroit Pistons of the National Basketball Association, averaging eight points and more than six rebounds per game as a part-time player.

Reed had a fine major league career, winning as many as 18 games in a season (1969), finishing in double figures in wins six times as a starter before becoming a highly successful reliever, mostly with the Phillies. Reed finished his career with 146 wins, and demonstrating his versatility, had 103 saves to go along with 55 complete games.

Interview with Ron Reed, July 19, 2023

Reed currently resides in Lilburn, Georgia, about 25 miles from where Atlanta Fulton-County Stadium stood. When I told him about the book I was writing on the night Henry Aaron hit #715, he was excited for the chance to speak with me about it, which we did over the phone.

Author: How did you feel going into the 715th game as the starting pitcher?

Reed: There was a lot of guessing going on at that time…Aaron got a lot of hate mail and a lot of crazy people in this world that didn't want to see a Black man from the South break a white icon's record. But we couldn't wait to see Hank start the season and work his way towards 715.

We opened the three-game series in Cincinnati and Opening Day, Hank was really nervous but in his first at-bat, he hit home run number 714. Yes, he was *real* nervous all right—but nerves didn't bother him at all!

It was his fourth game of the season when he hit home run 715. He was so happy to have that over with...the pressure of the people bugging him all the time.

Author: Was the hoopla surrounding home run 715 distracting you as you were pitching that game?

Reed: Not really because the feeling in that clubhouse was we just couldn't wait to see Hank hit 715. I was a teammate for seven years. I got to see this man play on a daily basis for seven years. Of course, I had to think about my job on the mound. But I wasn't really thinking about when he was going to hit 715. That didn't enter my mind. But as it worked out, we were all cheering hard for him the whole time. And man, when he hit that 715, and that stadium erupted, every player on that team was at home plate waiting for him.

Author: How about the Dodgers? Did it look like they were a little distracted?

Reed: I didn't get any particular type of feel of what was going on in their minds, other than when Hank hit the home run. When he went around the bases, each player at each base for the Dodgers gave him a high five or shook his hand or something. They all acknowledged him hitting the home run which you don't see that very often. So they were very aware of the moment. I was so into winning that game, and, of course as a pitcher, and watching Hank hit 715 that I didn't really pay that much attention to what was going on with the Dodgers.

Author: What about when Aaron hit the 715th home run, and you saw those kids run on the field, what entered your mind?

Reed: He got a lot of death threats during the off-season. The Braves had hired some security people to be around him in and out of the park. There were some rumors floating around that they might have even had a couple of Army guys stationed up on the roofs of the ballpark just in case someone would run out there on the field and attack Hank in any way, shape or form. That was a rumor, now I don't know if that was true or not, but that was a rumor. It's a home run, he's rounding second, and by shortstop these two guys run out on the field and they want to hug his neck and give him a high five. And I'm thinking, my gosh, if we've got snipers up there on the roof, those two guys are going to be in deep trouble if they're going after Hank. Of course, it didn't work out that way. I don't think there ever was anybody on the roof. But still, that rumor was floating around. My feeling was that when those guys ran out, they were lucky to get off this field alive if that was the case.

Author: Did you get a chance to talk to Hank either after the home run or after the game?

Reed: Not that particular night. I mean he had so many people around him, he had family and friends, and when he came into the clubhouse, I think they put him back in another room, he wasn't with the players in the clubhouse. There were so many people with cameras and microphones, and he was doing all kinds of interviews. Most of us were probably dressed and gone and that was still going on.

I saw a picture when Hank crossed home plate, I was one that got to him pretty much first...I was behind him and had my arms around him and stayed hugging his neck. I'm right there...being 6-5 at that time...I kinda stood above everybody else. I was so excited, of course, all the other players were going crazy! We had a very close-knit team with that '74 team, all the Braves teams I played with. I played with some really good guys...really team oriented. All of us were big Hank fans, no question about it.

Author: How did it feel to be the winning pitcher in such an historic game?

Reed: At the moment, you are so wrapped up in the game that you don't think that much about it until a few days later. Then you realize, gosh darn, I was the winning pitcher in a very historic game, a man breaks the all-time home run record. Later on, as the years have gone by, that moment to me seems to have gotten bigger and bigger. In fact, a lot of times when I talk to people and they say, did you play with the Braves, were you the pitcher that pitched the night that Hank...yeah, I was the winning pitcher when Hank hit 715, and I blow out my chest, and say, "Yes, sir, I was the winning pitcher that night!" I let everybody know that I was the winning pitcher the night Hank Aaron broke Babe Ruth's record, believe me!

I also was the starting and winning pitcher the night Hank hit home run number 500 and was the starting pitcher when Hank hit his 600th home run but I had to leave late in the game, and they tied it up.

***

Reed, a graduate of Notre Dame, played 19 seasons in the big leagues, winning a World Series Championship ring as a reliever with the Philadelphia Phillies in 1980 and retiring in 1984. He was inducted into the Toyota Phillies Wall of Fame in 2022.

Interview with Buzz Capra, who saved the game for Reed

Braves' relief pitcher Capra must have been inspired by Aaron as he became the 1974 National League earned run average (ERA) champion (2.28) and an All-Star. The 5'-11" righthander

1974 was memorable for Buzz Capra in many ways, as he moved into the rotation and finished the season with a league-leading ERA of 2.28 and 16 wins, more than half his career total of 31.
(Photo courtesy of Buzz Capra)

won nine straight games for Atlanta, having to fill in as a starter when Ron Reed broke his hand later in the season. He saved the game for starter/winning pitcher Reed, setting down nine of 10 batters in the last three innings, striking out six, as the Braves brought down the Los Angeles Dodgers by a score of 7-4.

"It was an exhilarating night," Capra told me. "I never thought I would be in that kind of situation."

According to Capra, he almost caught the 715th home run ball himself, but at the last-minute switched places with reliever Tom House who snagged the ball on the fly in the Braves' left-field bullpen. The relievers had placed themselves at 10-yard intervals in the area, wondering who might be the lucky one. The ball cleared the fence just a few feet above outfielder Bill

Buckner's glove, coming down in House's mitt right in front of the BankAmericard advertising sign that read: "Think of It as Money."

"715 was electrifying...we had hoped he was going to do it that night," Capra said. "We were all so excited. It goes without saying we figured he would pull the ball over the Cyclone fence to the relief pitchers. People in the stands began throwing stuff at me, ice cubes maybe. I ended up behind Tom House when he caught the ball."

When the players headed onto the field to greet Hank, "we were really pumped up."

"We were excited to greet him, but we also wanted to give him some space," Capra said.

"Thinking about it as the years go by, I was really thrilled to be a part of history."

When Capra visited the Baseball Hall of Fame, he said he was excited to see the Braves' lineup card from that night with his name on it in the "Hank Aaron Chasing the Dream" exhibit.

Sluggers (L-R) Joe Torre, Felipe Alou, Mack Jones, and Henry Aaron were four of six Braves to exceed 20 home runs in 1965. (Marion Johnson photographs, VIS 33.78.39, Kenan Research Center at Atlanta History Center)

Chapter Nine
715

Aaron's slow pre-at-bat ritual (shown here ahead of his first time up) contributed to the amazing concentration he achieved at the plate.
(Randy Cox)

Henry had arrived at the stadium around 4 PM after an afternoon of watching soap operas like "The Edge of Night" at his home in Southwest Atlanta. He loved watching westerns and soaps like "Edge," "As the World Turns," and "Secret Storm." Apparently, he was sorely ticked off when the network pulled the latter from the airways in the '70s.

Manager Eddie Mathews made sure all the annoying press folks were removed from the clubhouse one hour (instead of

Henry Aaron walks to the plate to lead off the fourth. (Randy Cox)

30 minutes) before game time to let Aaron and the other players prepare themselves mentally for what was to transpire in the next few hours.

No ballplayer had a closer look at Aaron's spectacular career than Eddie Mathews, as he and Hank belted 863 combined home runs as teammates, so the night must have had extra meaning for him. It was appropriate that Mathews serve as protector for Aaron as The Hammer approached the record in 1973 and for the big night in 1974. Aaron spoke fondly of Mathews after their careers were over, saying that when Aaron was young, Eddie "was one guy that took up for me more than anybody else on the Braves."

Mathews took up for Aaron as his manager as well. Starting in 1954, Aaron's rookie year, until Eddie was fired as the Braves skipper during the middle of the 1974 season, Mathews was cognizant of Aaron's "growing pains" in his early days as a rookie, and his development into the great player he became.

Mathews was given the chance to manage Aaron in 1972, taking over the Braves around midseason. In his first full year as manager, he rested Aaron regularly so he would be fresh when he did play. That year, The Hammer played in 120 games, about three out of four, especially welcome during the heat of the Atlanta summer. As noted, Mathews wanted to hold Henry out of the entire three-game series with Cincinnati on the road so he could tie and break Ruth's home run record at home in the 11-game homestand beginning on April 8.

Al Downing winds up. (Randy Cox)

"I did not consult Bill Bartholomay or Eddie Robinson before making my decision," Mathews said. "This is a decision I made on my own. I made this decision so Hank could have the opportunity to break the record in Atlanta."

Commissioner Kuhn had other ideas, and strongly suggested that Aaron should play in a "pattern" (two out of three games) as he did in 1973. So Aaron played in the first game, hitting the home run that tied Ruth's record at 714, sat out the second, but to avoid Bowie Kuhn's "serious consequences," Mathews complied and started Aaron in game 3, who went hitless, setting the stage for 715 in Atlanta.

"I hope the fans know me well enough to know that I play every game with everything I've got and I would never cut down or choke up on my swing to keep from breaking the record here," Aaron said before the series started.

The atmosphere at Fulton-County Stadium was electric as the crowd settled in, hoping to see history be made, as Aaron sought to achieve "the Cadillac of baseball records." Thunderous applause greeted him as he approached the plate, readying himself to meet his destiny in the form of a fastball from the Dodger hurler. I readied my camera and hoped that the time was right. We didn't notice the cold or rain.

After Aaron's first-inning walk, in which he did not swing the bat, the Dodgers plated three runs in the third and took that lead into the bottom of the fourth, when Bad Henry would bat again.

Before the game, Downing said he was going to pitch Aaron the same way he faced him before: changing locations and mixing up his pitches.

"It's no disgrace if I make a mistake," he said. "The pitcher who throws the LAST home run that Aaron hits will be remembered more so than the one who throws 715," Downing predicted. That was Dick Drago of the California Angels, who is considerably less remembered than Downing as it turns out.

At one point, Downing said the pressure really wasn't on him. "The pressure will be on the next guy," as he predicted (again incorrectly) that Aaron would go 0-for-4 against him and would have to get his 715th later.

"...I stayed up thinking about the pitcher I was going to face the next day...," Aaron wrote in his autobiography. "I used to play

Downing follows through. (Randy Cox)

every pitcher in my mind before I went to the ballpark." It was perhaps no different for him with Downing that night, though one has to wonder, with the eyes of the world on him, if he had been able to maintain his routine.

Darrell Evans led off the inning by reaching first on an error by shortstop Bill Russell. Aaron then slowly approached the plate, his extraordinary ability to concentrate being challenged by the size of the moment. He stepped in and began the ritual half-swings of his 35-inch, 33-ounce Louisville Slugger, awaiting the first pitch.

Downing's first delivery was down, but the next one caught too much of the plate and Aaron hammered the fastball over the left-center field fence for home run #715, a two-run masterpiece that traveled 400 feet through the cold, wet air, scoring Evans ahead of him. The time was 9:07 PM, April 8, 1974, incredibly, on his first swing of the night after hitting #714 on his first swing of the season four days earlier. A new Home Run King was crowned—Henry Louis Aaron.

I had been concentrating so hard on getting a photo of #715 that I almost didn't realize what had happened. I was just numb as the ball dropped into Tom House's glove and Aaron began his trot around the bases. Time stood still as the crowd exploded into exultation, with everyone cheering, clapping, and screaming like I'd never seen or heard before. There was a magical

King Henry gets his pitch and doesn't miss it, delivering home run #715 on his first swing of the game, just as he had done with #714. (Randy Cox)

feeling about the moment, that we had witnessed something superhuman, and that we were part of something bigger than baseball, that we were a part of history.

For me, I can't imagine experiencing a greater moment—my hero since 1957 doing what was once thought impossible, right before my eyes. I'd seen him in that first World Series, then homering in the 1969 playoffs, and belting #600, all of which paled in comparison to that moment.

Later, Downing said he wanted to keep the ball down and away but the ball drifted over the plate. "...I didn't think the pitch he hit was going out," he said, "but the ball just kept carrying and carrying...".

Because of its historic impact on American culture and the game of baseball, with the story unfolding and the drama building over a long period of time, the triumph of Henry Aaron is considered by many sports people, including the late Hall of Fame broadcaster Curt Gowdy, to be the "greatest sports story in history."

Braves radio broadcaster Milo Hamilton's call on number 715 went like this: "There's a drive into left-center field. That ball is going to be...out of here! It's gone! It's 715! There's a new Home Run Champion of all time! And it's Henry Aaron!"

As Aaron was greeted at home plate by his ecstatic teammates, Hamilton continued with: "Henry Aaron, the Home Run King of All Time."

Aaron heading to home plate, with Davey Johnson (6) waiting to greet him. (Randy Cox)

Gowdy's call on NBC television: "There's a long drive…the ball's hit deep…gone! He did it!! Aaron's the all-time home run leader…".

Vin Scully, doing the radio broadcast for the Dodgers, also had a memorable call: "To the fence. It is gone." Scully let his audience savor the moment with silence, after which he continued, "What a marvelous moment for baseball. What a marvelous moment for Atlanta and the state of Georgia. What a marvelous moment for the country and the world. A Black man is getting a standing ovation in the deep South for breaking a record of an all-time baseball idol."

The scoreboard, otherwise known as the Fan-O-Gram, lit up the Stadium when Aaron hit his home run, revealing the magic number: 715.

The moment was truly exhilarating, and the crowd had that same emotion. I didn't think the cheering would ever stop…ovation after ovation. People were watching all over the world on television, and Atlanta was the sports capital of the world and the center of the universe if just for a short time.

Home plate umpire, David Leroy "Satch" Davidson, watched The Hammer touch home plate to make things official. He noted later that if Aaron had taken the HR pitch, he probably would have called it a ball, though in the replay it appears the pitch caught plenty of the plate.

Davey Johnson was the first player to greet Aaron after he crossed the plate. Dusty Baker was on deck, and he gave the other players the opportunity to greet The Hammer before him. Perhaps because his relationship with Aaron was so special, he wanted to connect with him in a quieter moment. Dodgers' catcher Joe Ferguson stood by helplessly as catchers had done more than 700 times before. His consolation was that he was now a part of one of the greatest moments in the history of sports!

Aaron's adoring teammates swarm onto the field! (Randy Cox)

Cliff Courtenay and Britt Gaston were the two young men who seized the magical moment when the rest of the crowd watched the arc of Aaron's blast, leapt onto the field past mesmerized security, greeting Aaron as he rounded second with pats on the superstar's back. Aaron shrugged them off with his elbows in typically unflappable fashion and continued his triumphant tour around the bases.

It turns out they were college students from Waycross, Georgia. They spent a few hours in jail before being bailed out. Charges were dropped, and Aaron reunited with them in 1994 and 2010, although after the game he said he had no recollection of the boys while he rounded the bases. "I was in my own little world at the time," he said. I, for one, am glad of that. No one has ever been more deserving of a moment of pure elation and satisfaction than Aaron was then.

Courtenay attended the University of Georgia and became an optometrist in Valdosta, Georgia, and is now retired. He said

Braves catcher Johnny Oates makes his way through the crowd to shake The Hammer's hand. (Randy Cox)

they had not planned to leap onto the field, that "it was pretty spontaneous."

Britt Gaston also graduated from UGA. He lived in Waycross and South Carolina, where he owned a company called Regional Graphics. He died in 2011 after an extended illness.

Chapter Ten
Celebration Extraordinaire!

A hero's welcome for a genuine hero. (Randy Cox)

Few in the stadium were happier after 715 than Braves' relief pitcher Tom House, who caught Aaron's homer in the Braves' bullpen, and as promised, sprinted across the field to give it to him.

"I went and put it right in Hank's hand," he said after catching the homer on the fly. "It was an emotional moment for both me and Hank." "Thanks, kid," Aaron replied.

Aaron's pursuit of Babe Ruth's home run record had driven the passion of the nation, but for his teammates who watched

Aaron up close every day, a large dose of emotion was mixed in with the excitement and thrill.

House had compiled a record of 4-2 with four saves in 1973, and an ERA of 4.68. As was the case for Buzz Capra, 1974 turned out to be the finest year in House's career by far, as he went 6-2 with an ERA of 1.93, with 56 appearances and 102.2 innings pitched, all in relief. In Aaron's role as spokesman for the Magnavox Company, he told House he would receive a color television set for making the historic grab.

House had a solid major league career and achieved even greater fame with his development of techniques and training for pitchers that were considered unorthodox at the time but are now used widely in the sport.

Despite his success, it's unlikely that any moment in House's career either as a player or coach matched the thrill he felt when he caught the home run ball and handed it to Aaron. Such was the respect and admiration The Hammer held in all of baseball, especially among his teammates.

Sammy Davis, Jr. immediately offered $25,000 for the ball, but it was not for sale. Around that time, the versatile entertainer Davis had tried to put together a movie based on the life of Henry Aaron, but it never came to fruition.

The ball had been labeled "15-1" in indelible ink, marking it as the record-breaker for "the most honored statistic in sports." After a tour that included old Atlanta Stadium, the "715 ball" now resides at the Baseball Hall of Fame in Cooperstown, N.Y., on loan from the Atlanta Braves.

So, what happened to the 715 HR bat? John Holland, assistant clubhouse manager that night, related that his boss, Bill Acree, long-time equipment manager, told him to retrieve the bat and put it under lock and key.

"I was the next person to touch that bat after the historic home run, and it had the '44' that I had marked on the knob when it was new," Holland said.

U.S. Newspaper Headlines Proclaim 715 to the World

"Aaron Standard Time: Seven-Fifteen: Hank Hammers Past the Babe into History"

"Move Over, Babe! Hammerin' Hank Lives the Impossible"

"Aaron Conquers Mountaintop With 715"

"Aaron stands with immortals with 715th blast"

"History Is Made! Atlanta's Henry Aaron Smashes 715th Homer"

"Aaron Swats No. 715 to Break Ruth's Record"

"The Hammer Crowned New Sultan of Swat"

"Babe – move over for Hank Aaron: home run king calls his shot"

"Aaron 715 Does It! 'Thank God, It's All Over,' Sighs Henry"

"World Hears Shot: Hank Scales Ruth's Mountain"

"All-Time Homer King: Hank Spanks 715th; Now No. 1"

"Hank hits 715th homer on rainy night in Georgia

"Aaron finally escapes ghost of Babe Ruth"

"Aaron moves into lead with 715: 20-year chase ends for Braves' slugger"

"Atlanta Fans Welcome Henry's 715th: Ruth's Record Snapped With 4th-Inning Wallop"

After the game, not surprisingly, Downing was not very happy and had little to say.

"Go talk to Aaron, he's the one who hit the homer," he told reporters. With time, his view of the event softened.

"The pitch wasn't higher than I wanted," Downing said. "It was just too much over the plate. I think that if the pitch had been a little farther away, he might have been reaching for the ball. The thing you're dealing with is he's not a normal hitter, he's the greatest."

And so, Downing took his place in history with a group of pitchers/victims that includes Guy Bush (Ruth's 714 in 1935), Tom Zachary (Ruth's 60 in 1927), and Tracy Stallard (Roger Maris' 61 in 1961). The list could be longer if long-ball record breakers of the Steroid Era were included, such as those who surrendered historic blasts to Mark McGwire and Barry Bonds, but I'll refrain from doing that. For the record, Jesus Tinoco, formerly of the Texas Rangers, gave up Aaron Judge's 62nd home run of the 2022 season.

Amid the chaos and the jubilation in the moments after 715, Henry enjoys a congratulatory kiss from Billye. (Randy Cox)

With the incredible pressure lifted, Aaron can begin to enjoy his status as baseball's new Home Run King. (Randy Cox)

Hank's wife Billye was right there on the spot to see her husband hit the historic home run, along with Hank's parents, Herbert, Jr., and Estella Aaron. One of the lasting images of the turmoil around home plate is that of Estella clinging to her devoted hero son in a hug to end all hugs, with Henry smiling brightly, tears in his eyes.

In Jacksonville, Florida, Aaron's three youngest children, Hank, Jr., Lary, and Dorinda, were watching the game on television, as was his daughter Gaile, in Nashville, Tennessee.

It took more than 10 minutes for things to settle down on the field and in the stands, as the cheering, congratulations, and fireworks display continued. For a while we were all stuck in time, until everyone remembered it was only the fourth inning and the rest of the game had to be played.

As the electricity finally abated and calm returned to the ballpark, people looked at each other, still a bit stunned, perhaps wondering, did that really just happen? The score was now 3-3.

Henry made a beeline to his family and loved ones in the jubilant, magical moments after 715. (Randy Cox)

The moment proved too big for old pro Al Downing, who, when the game resumed, walked Dusty Baker and Davey Johnson in succession and was then replaced by that year's eventual Cy Young Award winner, Mike Marshall. Baker and Johnson came around to score, giving the Braves a lead that they would not relinquish. It might be said the entire Dodgers team was overwhelmed by the moment, as they committed six errors and a passed ball during the game!

Exodus to the Parking Lot?

There was a huge crowd for Aaron's record-breaking night but, according to some media accounts, about 20,000 of them left before the game was over.

```
LOS ANGELES            ATLANTA
         ab r h bi              ab r h bi
Lopes 2b  2 1 0 0  Garr rf      3 0 0 1
Lacy 2b   1 0 0 0  Lum 1b       3 0 0 1
Buckner lf 3 0 1 0 Evans 3b     4 1 0 0
Wynn cf   4 0 1 2  HAaron lf    3 2 1 2
Ferguson c 4 0 0 0 Office cf    0 0 0 0
WCrwfrd rf 4 1 1 0 Baker cf     2 1 1 0
Cey 3b    4 0 1 1  DaJohnsn 2b  3 1 1 0
Garvey 1b 4 1 1 0  Foster 2b    0 0 0 0
Russell ss 4 0 1 0 Correll c    4 1 0 0
Downing p 1 1 1 1  CRobinsn ss  0 0 0 0
Marshall p 1 0 0 0 Tepedino ph  0 0 0 1
Joshua ph 1 0 0 0  MPerez ss    2 1 1 0
Hough p   0 0 0 0  Reed p       2 0 0 0
Mota ph   1 0 0 0  Oates ph     1 0 0 1
                   Capra p      0 0 0 0
          -------                
Total     44 4 7 4 Total        9 7 4 6
Los Angeles        003 001 000 — 4
Atlanta            010 402 00x — 7
```

E—Buckner, Cey, Russell 2, Lopes, Ferguson. LOB—Los Angeles 5, Atlanta 7. 2B—Baker, Russell, Wynn. HR—H.Aaron (2). S—Garr. SF—Garr.

```
                 IP   H  R ER BB SO
Downing (L,0-1)  3    2  5  2  4  2
Marshall         3    2  2  1  1  1
Hough            2    0  0  0  2  1
Reed (W,1-0)     6    7  4  4  1  4
Capra            3    0  0  0  1  6
```

Save—Capra (1). WP—Reed. PB—Ferguson. T—2:27. A—53,775.

The box score: Aaron's season home run total stood at two, two of the most important long balls in baseball history. (Public Domain)

Braves stars Henry Aaron, Eddie Mathews, and Tony Cloninger visit children at a local hospital in October 1965. (Marion Johnson photographs, VIS 33.67.27, Kenan Research Center at Atlanta History Center)

Chapter Eleven
True Greatness

As part of the post-home run ceremony and celebration for Aaron, Bill Bartholomay presented him a ring inscribed with the numeral "715" on it, calling him "the greatest player to ever play the game of baseball." Aaron's "speech" in the aftermath was short, sweet, and characteristically honest: "I just thank God it's over."

Aaron's teammates get a chance to speak with him in a quiet moment after the game. (Randy Cox)

The electronic Fan-O-Gram flashed a message honoring the "Sultan of Swat": "George Herman Ruth also shares this great moment with all of us tonight – by setting the standard of 714 which made the great chase possible."

Henry received many telephone calls after he hit Number 715: his children, of course, but he also heard from President Richard Nixon after Donald Davidson had accidentally cut him off on the transfer call to the clubhouse; and Commissioner Kuhn, who, as mentioned earlier, had opted to attend a Wahoo Club dinner in Cleveland rather than attending the big game in Atlanta. On the menu might have been roast beef, but it probably tasted like crow! In his place, he sent his promotion assistant, Monte Irvin, a National League Hall of Famer with the New York Giants, who presented Aaron with a $3,000 diamond-encrusted wristwatch with Number "715" embossed in gold. Later, Irvin told reporters that his boss should have been there.

Here's how I described the aftermath of Aaron's home run in my book, *A Baby Boomer's Guide to Collecting Comic Books and Baseball Cards,* "When Aaron finished circling the bases, some of the reporters and most of the photographers, me included, poured onto the field to take part in a slice of sports history. The biggest thrill for me was talking to Aaron after he hit the home run and shaking his hand."

Always the consummate team player, Aaron spoke to the media after the game, telling them that he was happy his home run contributed to the Braves' 7-4 victory over the Dodgers. "The win is the most important thing that happened tonight," he said.

Six-Year Appearance Feud

The Aaron-Kuhn feud had been simmering for a while, but it became red-hot in Cincinnati when Kuhn ordered the Braves to play the slugger in the Sunday game, and intensified when the commissioner was a no-show on the night of #715.

Six years later, in January 1980, another salvo was fired, as The Hammer refused to accept an award Kuhn wanted to present to him for delivering the "greatest moment of the decade in the 1970s." The *Baseball Magazine*-sponsored awards had selected the Reds' Pete Rose as the "player of the decade," and that didn't sit too well with Aaron. He said his achievements "overshadowed anything anyone else did," saying that Kuhn's absence on April 8, 1974 was an insult to Atlanta fans and himself but it was an even bigger slap to ask him "... to get up on that podium...".

Reconciliation may have begun the next month, when Kuhn asked for a confab with the Home Run King in New York in the hopes of patching things up. After the meeting, Aaron said both parties were satisfied with the results of the "cordial and fruitful" meeting. In addition to the two men discussing Kuhn's absence on the night of #715 and his unhappiness with Aaron snubbing Kuhn at the 1970s award show, Aaron also expressed his frustration with the low number of African Americans in managerial and executive positions in baseball.

Postgame press conference with Henry and Billye. (Randy Cox)

"I feel that I can have a great season now," he commented, adding that both he and his teammates could relax now that the home run chase was over.

The home run, Aaron said, was a bit of a surprise. "I wasn't sure I hit that ball hard enough for it to go out," he commented. He normally didn't watch his home runs soar through the air, but this one, he said, he watched!

Aaron said that the record-breaker felt "just like another home run," and he had predicted if he was thrown a strike, he could hit one out. "I just wanted to touch all the bases on this one," he related. "I'll probably wake up in the morning and realize what has happened then."

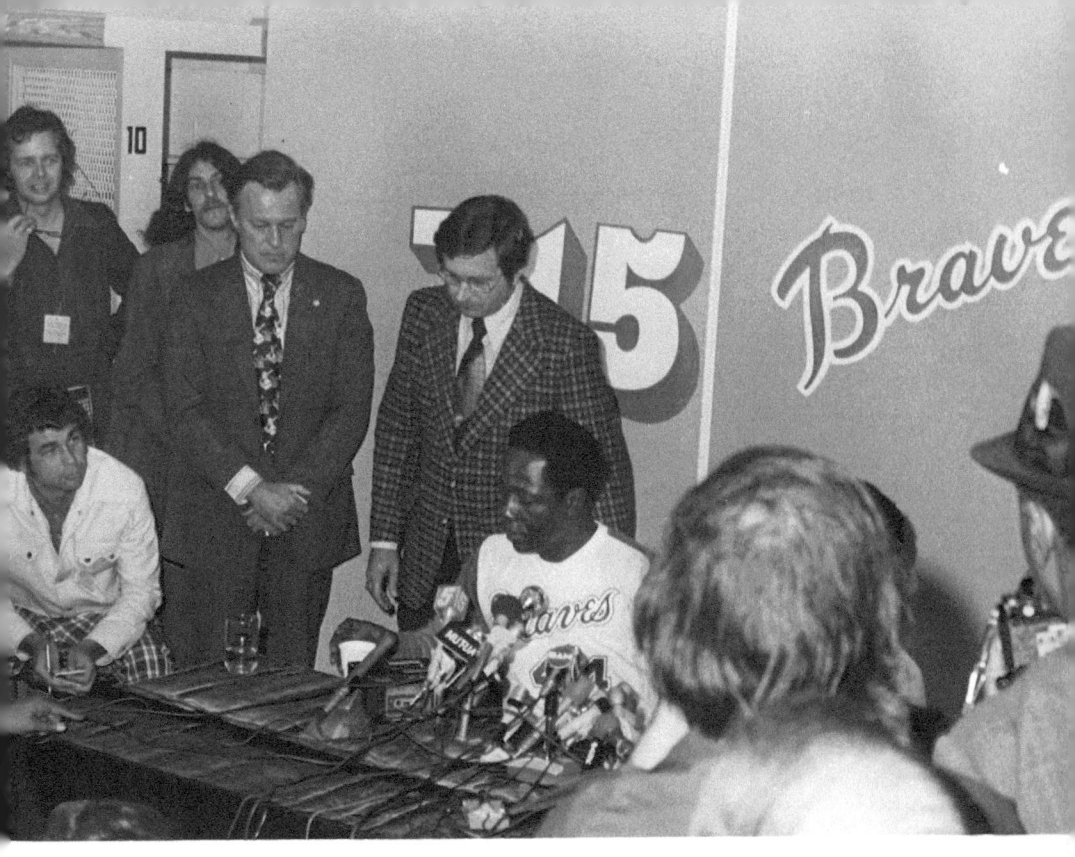

Media from around the world surrounded Henry during the post-game press conference. (Randy Cox)

Re-enacting 715 and Celebrating the 40th Anniversary

On April 8, 1984, 10 years to the night that Aaron broke Ruth's record, the Atlanta Braves decided to stage a re-enactment of that great feat. Hank was ready, and so was pitcher Al Downing. The stage was set for a pre-game event before threatening skies and only about 10,000 fans who also came to see the Montreal Expos.

Aaron said it was challenging to go up against Downing 10 years later, even though he imagined it couldn't have been easy for Downing either, though all the pressure was on Aaron to hit.

> "I thought the ball I hit was a 92 mile-per-hour fastball," Hank joked about the home run he clubbed to just about the same place as #715 had gone. This time, however, it took him 16 pitches to knock one out of the park!
>
> On April 9, 2014, Henry and Atlanta Braves fans celebrated 715's 40th anniversary at Turner Field, as 715 fans stood out in center field, each holding a sign representing one of the slugger's home runs.
>
> That night, Aaron said he appreciated the kindness fans showed him for the past 40 years and that for his entire major league career, he "gave baseball everything that I had, every ounce of my abilities to play the game. I tried to play to make you, the fans, appreciate me more," he said.

The Hammer finished the 1974 season with 20 home runs and 69 RBIs in 340 at-bats – solid production – and was traded to the Milwaukee Brewers (managed by his old teammate, catcher Del Crandall) in the off-season. The move to the American League allowed Aaron to continue his career, playing primarily as designated hitter in his final two seasons. In 1975 and 1976, Aaron tacked on another 22 home runs, to finish his illustrious career with 755 home runs in the city where it all began, just as Babe Ruth had done, who started with the Boston Red Sox and finished with the Boston Braves.

In his remarkable 23-year career, Henry Louis Aaron compiled an unprecedented record of achievements in Major League Baseball: first in runs batted in, with 2,297; total bases, with 6,856; extra-base hits, with 1,477, and All-Star Game appearances, with 25. He played in two All-Star games in both 1959 and 1960. His career batting average was .305 (.310 in his years with the Braves). And as testament to Aaron's ability to hit in the clutch, his career batting average with runners in scoring position was .326.

Aaron ranks second in home runs (755) behind Barry Bonds' 762 and times at bat (12,364); third in hits (3,771) and games played (3,298); and tied with Ruth for fourth in runs scored (2,174). He led his league in homers and RBIs four times, captured two batting titles, and won three Gold Gloves for fielding excellence. He hit 44 homers each of four years: 1957, 1963, 1966, and 1969, blasted 45 in 1962 and 47 (his highest total) in 1971. In addition, he whacked 624 doubles, 98 triples, stole 240 bases, walked 1,402 times (compared with 1,383 strikeouts), and had an OPS (on base average plus slugging) of .928. That figure, achieved in a largely pitching-dominant era, yielded a career OPS of 155, meaning that Aaron's overall production was 55% better than the major league average.

Looking at another relatively new statistic, Henry Aaron's career total WAR (Wins Above Replacement) is 143.0, seventh highest all time. To put that number in perspective, only 21 position players totaled as many as 100 WAR, and only 60 all time have HALF as many as Aaron.

Public Recognition

Public recognition nationwide was very slow for The Hammer, especially compared to contemporaries like Mickey Mantle and Willie Mays, who both played in big media markets like New York and San Francisco. In 1969, as the story goes, there was a glimmer of recognition for Aaron in Houston at the home of Tal Smith, director of player personnel for the Astros. Smith's home had been burglarized, and the culprits saw two baseballs, one autographed by Mays and the other by Aaron, sitting together. The bad guys took the Aaron ball and left the one of Mays.

The Giants and Braves were in a fight to the finish to win the first ever National League West title in 1969, with the Bravos capturing it. This turned out to be Aaron's final postseason appearance.

Inside the Home Run Numbers

At one point before belting #715 Aaron was asked to name the top ten home runs of his career. This was the list he provided.

His **Number 1** most memorable home run clinched the 1957 National League pennant, a two-run blast off St. Louis' Billy Muffett (who later pitched for the Atlanta Crackers) in extra innings on September 23 at Milwaukee's County Stadium.

Number 2 came on July 14, 1968, in Atlanta: Aaron became the eighth player in major league history to hit 500 career home runs. With Felipe Alou and Felix Millan on base, Hank cranked one out against Mike McCormick of the San Francisco Giants, hitting the Fan-o-Gram board in left-center field.

Number 3: Hank's two-run homer off Gaylord Perry on July 25, 1972, in the first All-Star Game hosted in the Southeast at Atlanta-Fulton County Stadium and, incredibly, his first home run in All-Star Game competition.

Number 4: As a rookie, his first home run in the major leagues, off Vic Raschi of the St. Louis Cardinals in Busch Stadium on April 23, 1954.

Number 5: Tying the record for Most Home Runs up to June 30, Hank hit his 24th four-bagger off Larry Jackson of the Philadelphia Phillies on June 21, 1966, at Atlanta Stadium. Aaron said: "As far as home runs are concerned, that's the hottest streak I've ever had."

Number 6: His last Milwaukee Braves' home run in County Stadium, off the Phillies' Ray Culp, on September 20, 1965.

Number 7: The day Aaron hit three homers in one game, the only time in his career he ever did that. It came on June 21, 1959, at Seal Stadium against the Giants. The unlucky pitchers were Johnny Antonelli, Stu Miller, and Gordon Jones.

Number 8: The 400th HR of his career came against Bo Belinsky in the ninth inning at Connie Mack Stadium against the Philadelphia Phillies, April 20, 1966.

Number 9: The home run that won him his first HR crown was memorable: a grand slammer off Sam Jones of the Cardinals. Bill Bruton, Johnny Logan, and Eddie Mathews were on base in the September 24, 1957, game. It was Hank's first grand slam of his career, his 44th home run of the season.

Number 10: Aaron swatted a 470-foot grand slam homer into the distant center-field bleachers at the Polo Grounds against the Mets on June 18, 1962. In the more than 40-year history of Major League Baseball at the Polo Grounds, Aaron's blast is one of only three to be hit there. Joe Adcock of the Braves and a young Lou Brock of the Cubs belted the others.

When Aaron smashed his 700th home run on July 21, 1973, off the Phillies' Ken Brett at Atlanta Stadium, Braves officials immediately painted a red hammer on the back of the seat where the home run ball landed, according to Bob Hope. Commissioner Kuhn didn't telephone Hank to congratulate him, saying he was waiting for his 715th to be there in person.

Robert Winborne, a sophomore at the University of North Carolina, was the lucky guy in the left-field stands to retrieve the ball, and, for his efforts, he collected $700 (in silver dollars). Only 2,000 fans attended the game.

The crowd is on its feet again, this time hoping to see home run #716. (Randy Cox)

Aaron hit 512 home runs in games his teams won, and 242 in games his teams lost. One home run was clobbered in a tie game. His best inning to hit HR's was the first: 124.

Aaron would have finished his career with 756 home runs if not for a bizarre and one might say horrible call in a game between the Braves and Cardinals in August of 1965. In the eighth inning of a 3-3 game, Aaron, frustrated by an endless diet of floating change-ups from long-time nemesis Curt Simmons, reached far for one and hit it 450 feet onto the roof of Sportsman's Park. Catcher Tim McCarver pointed to where Aaron's front foot allegedly landed (out of the batter's box), which home plate umpire Chris Pelekoudas bought into, declaring Aaron out. Aaron was livid, and manager Bobby Bragan got ejected for arguing. Years later, the Cards' Bob Uecker, one-time Atlanta Cracker and long-time friend of Henry, said, "It's one of the few times I ever saw Aaron blow his stack." The Braves protested the game, but then won on a home run in the ninth by long-forgotten Don Dillard, so the protest became moot.

Hank's Statistical Legacy

The game of baseball lives and breathes by its statistics, and Henry Aaron provided enough to keep any accountant working 24 hours a day:

> *** Hank and Tommie Aaron both hit homers in the same inning on July 12, 1962, to whip the Cardinals, 8 to 6. Tommie clubbed a solo homer, and his brother topped things off with a walk-off grand slam in the bottom of the ninth.

> *** Although the St. Louis Cardinals' Bob Gibson gave The Hammer fits at the plate, he still cracked eight dingers off him, the most Gibson allowed to a right-handed hitter.

> ***In contrast, Aaron hit a remarkable .362 against Sandy Koufax in 116 at-bats, and struck out only 12 times against "The Left Arm of God," less than once per every 10 plate appearances.

> ***Aaron also feasted on another flame-throwing lefty, Don Gullet. Gullet, who didn't break into the majors until 1970 when Aaron was 36, finished his injury-shortened career with a sparkling record of 109-50. In his career against Gullet, Aaron went 12-for-26, with nine bases of balls and SEVEN home runs!

> *** The Hammer showed perseverance, longevity, and consistency by blasting 20-plus homers in 20 seasons, another MLB record.

> *** The only inside-the-park homer Aaron ever hit came on May 10, 1967, against Jim Bunning of the Philadelphia Phillies.

*** Aaron, Eddie Mathews, Joe Adcock, and Frank Thomas were the first foursome to hit back-to-back-to-back-to-back home runs, in 1961.

*** Hank would remain in the 3,000-hit club even if you took away all his home runs, which, of course, you can't do, and wouldn't want to. But it's a tribute to what a great all-around hitter he was.

*** *The Sporting News* ranked Henry Louis Aaron fifth on their 100 greatest players' list, in 1999.

Non-Statistical Honors

Wisconsin Governor Jim Doyle in 2006 helped Hank dedicate the Henry Aaron State Trail that connects Miller Park in Milwaukee with Lake Michigan.

Hank found time as a youth to achieve the rank of Eagle Scout, In addition, he received the Lifetime Achievement Award from the Boy Scouts of America.

Henry was a guest on the CBS-TV children's show "Captain Kangaroo" in 1957, his first on national television in a non-baseball appearance.

Nelson Briles, a pitcher with the Pittsburgh Pirates, composed and recorded a song which he hoped would ward off the inevitable: facing The Hammer. His was one of several written about the future home run king and was produced by Tony Butala, lead singer of The Lettermen for Capitol Records.

It was called, "Hey, Hank, I Know You're Goin' T' Do It, But Please Don't Hit It Off Me."

Here's how it went:

"PLEASE!

I've got a reputation.

And I've got a fam-i-ly

So please don't hit it

So please don't hit it

So please don't hit it off me!"

It turned out Briles had nothing to worry about since he was traded to the Kansas City Royals in the American League in the winter of 1973, but he did end up rerecording a more generic version for the public.

Pitchers who DID have to face Aaron naturally weren't too happy about it. Two of his favorites were Don Drysdale and Claude Osteen of the L.A. Dodgers. Drysdale gave up 17 gopher balls to Hank, and Osteen 14. Osteen had this to say about the Man from Mobile: "Slapping a rattlesnake across the face with the back of your hand is safer than trying to fool Henry Aaron."

Pirates ace hurler Bob Friend offered up 12 home runs while the following pitchers surrendered 10 each: Don Cardwell of five teams, including the Braves; Roger Craig of the Dodgers and N.Y. Mets; and Larry Jackson of the St. Louis Cardinals, Chicago Cubs, and Philadelphia Phillies. Altogether, Aaron hit four-baggers off 310 pitchers. Teamwise, the Reds were his favorite target; they were victimized 97 times. He hit 534 off right-handers, 221 off lefties.

Number 715 really could come at any moment, and Philadelphia Phillies pitcher Curt Simmons was a true believer, saying "throwing a fast ball by Henry Aaron is like trying to sneak the sun past a rooster." Aaron often cited Simmons as one of the toughest pitchers he had to face (despite Simmons being a lefty), and the numbers bear it out. Bad Henry was limited to six long balls against him and a batting average of .268.

When the baseball season began in the spring of 1974, the Magnavox Corporation, makers of televisions and other appliances at the time, and the Atlanta Braves published what they called the *Hank Aaron Sportscaster's Statistical Guide* as a tribute to his and Ruth's outstanding contributions to baseball. The guide listed their individual home run records, along with biographical information.

Aaron grounded out his last two at-bats in the 715 game before being replaced in left field to another long, thunderous ovation. (Randy Cox)

Bob Hope and the public relations staff of the Braves put in some long hours because they were really covering two entities: the Atlanta Braves and Henry Louis Aaron.

One of its major sections featured quotations from The Hammer himself, giving insight into what he was having to endure:

"I know what I am attempting to accomplish will be an example for every kid, Black or white, in whatever they do."

"I want to be remembered as a player who hit for average, stole bases, and did everything a complete ballplayer should." Aaron credited Braves manager Bobby Bragan with encouraging him to steal more bases.

"When the final curtain comes down, my record will speak for itself."

> "I've found out that the best thing for Henry Aaron to do is to go out there every day, do the best he can and let the chips fall where they may. I have a lot of respect for whomever is on the mound any given day, and I hope he feels the same about me."
>
> Henry Aaron

In the stats guide distributed to countless media outlets following the home run chase, many players and others had pertinent things to say about Hank:

"The Babe loved baseball so very much. I know he would be pulling for Hank Aaron to break his record."

Mrs. Babe Ruth

"It feels so great that so many love Henry enough to get up and cheer for him. It was wonderful."

Estella Aaron, Henry's mother

"I've never seen so much excitement in a crowd. I don't think there could be that much for a

World Series. I got goose bumps every time he came up."

Atlanta Braves Pitcher Phil Niekro

"When I arrive in our dugout in Atlanta, I start looking for Hank. I guess I'm hoping I don't see him."

Pittsburgh Pirates Pitcher Steve Blass

"If he breaks Ruth's record, and it looks as if he will, I say it has to be the greatest accomplishment in the entire history of sports."

Boston Red Sox Outfielder Carl Yastrzemski

"I like Hank Aaron. I still feel that way. As far as I'm concerned, Aaron is the best ballplayer of my era. He is to baseball of the last 15 years what Joe DiMaggio was before him."

New York Yankees Outfielder Mickey Mantle

"People ask me if Hank has changed since he came up in '54. I say outside of maturing, not at all. His hat size hasn't changed an eighth of an inch."

Braves Pitcher and Coach Lew Burdette

Here is a sampling of some of the things Henry Aaron's fans wrote to their hero during the chase for 715, as captured by the Braves' PR Department.

Kids' Quotes:

"You swing the bat around like an angry elephant. They couldn't strike you out with a ping pong ball, you would hit that, too. So, let's do it, Hank, 715 here we come!!!"

P.B., Philadelphia, Pa.

"I'm glad you are on our side. You are the best baseball player in the whole small world!"

H.D., Decatur, Ga.

"I know this sounds silly, but when you hit your 714 home run do you think after that game you could send me a piece of dirt that was in your baseball shoes or your shoe lace or a piece of your uniform?"

B.R., Paramus, N.J.

"Could you send me a penny? Because I would like to see what Georgia money looks like."

K.L., Attica, N.Y.

"I want an autographed ball, Mr. Aaron, this is a school project. Please send it fast because whoever wins gets free ice cream for a week."

S.R., Poquoson, Va.

"I am glad that you hit 711 home runs. You are almost up with baby root. I hope you will catch baby root."

C.F., Los Angeles, Cal.

Adult fans also had strong opinions about Aaron:

"This country should be honored that you became a part of a sport that so many love. You are a great man because of what you are, not because you can hit baseballs."

C.H., Columbus, Ga.

"We admire your fortitude, courage, and are grateful for the inspiration you have given to many people over our land, as well as around the world. You have reminded us again and again that true greatness is a matter of attitude and motive."

M.L., Goshen, Iowa

"I have a son who is two years old. Someday he may be watching someone trying to break your record and ask me, 'Did you watch Hank Aaron?' I will say, 'Yes, he was a man respected by both white and Black alike, not only as a great ballplayer, but also a proud and humble man, dedicated not only to the sport in which he played, but mankind itself.'"

D.R., Gallitzin, Pa.

"I want to say that I respect and admire you as a man with great dignity, and as a model for all Americans. When I have a son, I will tell him of you and hope that he may emulate you and learn from you the many qualities that you possess. You are a great man."

F.F., Liverpool, N.Y.

"On the day you hit your 700th home run, my wife had a baby boy. Because of our great respect for you as a ballplayer and as a person, we have chosen the name Aaron, in your honor."

D.S., Dayton, Ohio

Chapter Twelve
A Hall of Fame Life

Always the perfect gentleman, Aaron had to tolerate a tremendous amount of racial prejudice during his pursuit of Babe Ruth's home run record. Throughout, he unfailingly remained dignified and professional, no matter how insensitive reporters' questions were and no matter what abuse was hurled his way by fans.

Early in his career, Aaron said little and chose his words carefully, which led him at times to be painted by the media as inarticulate or reticent. Resentments developed on both sides of the relationship, though as the years went by, both grew more comfortable with the other.

As people realized The Hammer had a chance to surpass Ruth's record, the spotlight intensified 100-fold. Aaron began receiving so much fan mail in 1973 that he was allowed to hire his own secretary as part of his contract. The daunting task of reading and answering his mountains of mail fell to Carla Koplin. Most fans supported and encouraged Henry. But as is well known, a small percentage were vicious and full of hate, some even threatening his life. Eventually, the volume of mail Aaron received made it impossible for them all to be answered.

The United States Postal Service estimated delivery of 930,000 fan letters to Henry during his career…more mail than any non-politician in history.

In 1973, Henry had to endure verbal harassment from belligerent home-town fans behind him in right field. No doubt the same was true on the road. During one game in Atlanta it became too much and he shouted back. "Sure, I was ready to fight," he said after the game. "All I want is to be treated like a human being…I've been the target of hatred and resentment. I've been getting it in hate letters, postcards and in abuse from the stands. They are a small minority but they're there just the same."

Some bigoted fans didn't like Aaron as the first Black superstar on the first major league team in the southeast, much less the one who was destined to smash Ruth's home run record.

Jackie Robinson: Aaron's Idol

After the young Aaron saw Jackie Robinson play, he knew that he had found his idol in the Brooklyn Dodger, who broke the color line in 1947. Aaron wanted to emulate Robinson's tremendous work ethic and follow in his footsteps. And that's just what he did.

After a spectacular stint as an All-American halfback at UCLA, Robinson spent three years in the U.S. Army during WWII and then turned to baseball in 1945, playing for the Kansas City Monarchs of the Negro American League. From there, Brooklyn Dodgers' GM Branch Rickey signed Robinson and sent him to their AAA affiliate, the Montreal Royals, where Robinson hit a sparkling

.349. The next year Jackie was called up to the Majors, and history was made.

Although Robinson was under tremendous pressure, he was ready for it. "...this is what I've been waiting for," he said. It was reported that years later Rickey offered the Braves $150,000 for Aaron, but that deal didn't happen.

When Robinson got his chance, sportswriters in New York and elsewhere were hailing him as "the Joe Louis of Baseball," referring to the heavyweight boxing champion of that era. Jackie was an amazing champion as well, performing magnificently until his retirement before the 1957 season.

Henry and Jackie competed against each other in the mid-1950s. In one game, Aaron came to bat with Robinson playing third base, as the Dodgers' defense set up for his power. Hank countered with a fake bunt, but Robinson didn't flinch. After the game, he asked Robinson why he didn't move. "We'll give you first base anytime you want," he said. There was mutual respect and admiration.

In 1949, Robinson played in a landmark game that would be a harbinger to Aaron's 715th home run night, as the Brooklyn Dodgers visited Ponce de Leon Ballpark in Atlanta to take on the Crackers in an exhibition game. In his first at-bat, Robinson received a standing ovation from the 15,000 hometown fans, as he broke the color barrier in playing for a white team against another white team in the South.

"This is the most thrilling experience of my life...it's great to feel that I am playing a part in breaking down the barrier against the people of my race," he said. "I was afraid it would never be in my lifetime."

He said he received his best reception on the team's tour earlier in Macon, Georgia. "It proved to me then and there that Georgia sports fans are no different from any other. All sports fans are alike regardless of what section of the country they come from," he said.

A quarter of a century later, Aaron continued Jackie's legacy with the home run chase and the breaking of Ruth's record.

Besides making the All-20th Century Baseball Team, Jackie was the first Black player to win the National League Most Valuable Player award in 1949. He sported a career batting average of .311 with 137 home runs, 734 runs batted in, 1,158 hits, and 947 runs scored in 10 seasons.

Robinson withstood racial prejudice and hostility without protests or recriminations, first with the Dodgers' farm club in Montreal, then with the parent team. He blazed the same kind of path with his impeccable conduct and integrity in and out of competition as Joe Louis, a former resident of LaFayette, Alabama, before him, and Hank Aaron afterwards.

Asked to sum up Robinson's skill, Rickey said he was "a beautiful hitter."

His aggressive baserunning was also unique, and helped transform the station-to-station style of baseball in the 1950s to a speed and stolen base style that became a big part of 1960s and 1970s baseball.

In his autobiography, *I Had a Hammer* (with Lonnie Wheeler), Aaron said that he wanted to follow in the path of legendary Jackie Robinson – to keep swinging at fastballs and bigotry.

"As a ballplayer, I always figured that I had a bat and all the pitcher had was a little ball, and as long as I kept swinging that bat I'd be all right," he wrote.

At some point in his career, Aaron decided to do something about easing some of this racial tension by a little subterfuge. When he checked into a hotel, he would book two rooms, one under his real name (unused) and the other under an alias: "A. Diefendorfer," which he occupied.

Another means to "get away" from the never-ending press coverage and public attention consisted of relaxing on his boat in Mobile Bay with friends and relatives. Aaron was not much of a swimmer so he always sported a life jacket, but he enjoyed the peace and calmness of the ocean on the two boats he owned, especially in the off-season of 1973.

Unfortunately for Aaron, he entrusted a significant amount of money to unnamed "investment bankers" who instead pocketed the money and left town without a trace. It was reported that Aaron lost nearly one million dollars to the thieves. Luckily, later on, great fortune on the field led to great financial fortune off the field.

Late in 1973, when Aaron signed the record $1 million, five-year contract with the Magnavox Corporation, it was the richest endorsement ever offered to an athlete. "...I've had opportunities to get associated with different companies, but for some reason things just didn't work out," Aaron said. "Now that things are beginning to pay off for me, I'm very pleased."

Aaron said that he enjoyed memorable visits to Los Angeles, where he was greeted by 50,000 fans, and to New York, where he met and rode in a motorcade parade through Harlem with Mrs. Babe Ruth and Mrs. Lou Gehrig.

For the 25th anniversary of his 715th homer, Major League Baseball honored Hank with the creation of an award given to the MLB's top hitter, naming it the "Hank Aaron Award." In 2002, President George W. Bush awarded The Hammer with the nation's highest civilian honor, the Presidential Medal of Freedom, for his humanitarian and philanthropic efforts. The NAACP created the "Hank Aaron Humanitarian in Sports Award," and its Legal Defense Fund named him the recipient of the Thurgood Marshall Lifetime Achievement Award in 2005.

A fantastic evening comes to end! (Randy Cox)

Henry Louis Aaron was not only the ultimate complete ballplayer, he was a champion of civil rights' causes throughout his life. His hero, Jackie Robinson, set an example for him early in life. "His courage and intelligence showed what the Black man could be made of," Aaron said.

Early in his career, Aaron was vocal in getting hotels to allow Black players the right to stay with their white teammates. Civil rights legislation was the catalyst for this movement, not from anything baseball had done, he said. Later in his career, Aaron decried the lack of Black coaches and executives in Baseball.

Besides Robinson, Dr. Martin Luther King, Jr. was one of Hank's heroes, a man who "could walk with kings and talk with presidents," a man years ahead of his time, he said.

> "On the field, Blacks have been able to be super giants. But, once our playing days are over, that is the end of it, and we go back to the back of the bus again."
>
> Henry Louis Aaron

His goal throughout his lifetime was to give young Black kids hope, showing by his actions that it takes discipline and staying power to do whatever you want to do in life. Before he died, Robinson gave him the advice to "keep the pressure on" or become complacent in what you're doing.

With the Milwaukee Braves, Aaron and teammate Bill Bruton supported candidates like John F. Kennedy and pressured Braves' officials to have "race signs" removed from Bradenton Park, the Spring Training facility near Sarasota, Florida.

He organized the Hank Aaron Celebrity Pro-Am Bowling Tournament, first held on November 14, 1972, in Atlanta, with $25,000 in donations going to sickle cell anemia research and testing.

The annual Elite Development Invitational was rebranded as The Hank Aaron Invitational. In it, 44 of the best minority high school ballplayers participate in a game at Truist Park in Atlanta as part of Hank Aaron Week in front of baseball scouts and college recruiters.

Players also received a week to experience the Jackie Robinson Training complex in Florida, and a tour of the MLK Center, King's home, and the Ebenezer Baptist Church in Atlanta. The Braves

44 Classic at Coolray Field (Gwinnett Stripers, Lawrenceville, Georgia) showcases a pro-style workout and ballgame in the two-day event for young ballplayers in the southern area.

In recent years, the Henry Louis Aaron Fund was established within the Atlanta Braves Foundation to boost minority participation in baseball, having received an initial allotment of $1 million from the players' association and the MLB. The 755 Legacy Club and the Henry Aaron Fellowship are also committed to honoring his life.

Aaron contributed to other civil rights causes outside of the spotlight, sometimes involving teammates or other players. He was a philanthropist, business owner, and humanitarian, besides being such a great role model to children and adults everywhere.

Aaron not only changed the game forever with his work ethic, consistency, and his God-given ability to play baseball, but his humanitarian efforts after he stopped playing have left an enduring legacy to the sports community and the world.

"I just want to hit 715 home runs and let the fans do what they want with the figures. They can argue about the lively ball, the longer schedule, more at bats, better fielding, or anything else they want to argue about," Aaron said. "I don't want anyone to forget Babe Ruth. I just want them to remember Hank Aaron."

The Atlanta Braves issued this statement on the death of the Home Run King:

> "...he was a beacon for our organization first as a player, then with player development, and always with our community efforts. His incredible talent and resolve helped him achieve the highest accomplishment, yet he never lost his humble nature.

Henry Louis Aaron wasn't just our icon, but one across Major League Baseball and around the world. His success on the diamond was matched only by his business accomplishments off the field and capped by his extraordinary philanthropic efforts."

Henry Louis Aaron passed away of natural causes on January 22, 2021. His death was mourned throughout the baseball world and beyond, and his life and achievements will be remembered forever.

Henry poses with his 1957 Most Valuable Player Award trophy, the only one of his career, a year in which his 132 RBIs were 27 more than the next best total in the National League.
(Joe McTyre photographs, VIS 106.01.01, Kenan Research Center at Atlanta History Center)

Bibliography

24/7 Sports web page, https://247sports.com/, article, "MLB Legend Hank Aaron dies at 86," by Nick Kosko, January 22, 2021.

150 Years of Braves Baseball, Skybox Press, China, 2020.

755 Homeruns.com web page, www.755homeruns.com/, articles, Hank Aaron Biography," by Dennis Yuhasz, "Hank Aaron Timeline," and "Hank Aaron versus Major League Pitchers."

1965 Braves Yearbook, Milwaukee Braves Public Relations Department, Milwaukee, Wisconsin, February 13, 1965.

1965 Milwaukee Braves Scorecard, Milwaukee Braves, Milwaukee, Wisconsin, August 1, 1965.

1966 Braves Scorebook, Atlanta Braves, Atlanta, Ga., April 23, 1966.

1967 Atlanta Braves Scorebook, Atlanta Braves, Atlanta, Georgia, 1967.

1969 National League Championship Series, Atlanta Braves vs. New York Mets, Official Program, Atlanta Braves Public Relations Department, Atlanta, Georgia, October 1, 1969.

1974 Guide for Press, Radio, and Television, Atlanta Braves Public Relations Department, Atlanta, Georgia, February 7, 1974.

1974 Hank Aaron Press, Radio, and TV Guide, Atlanta Braves Public Relations Department, Atlanta, Georgia, February 7, 1974.

Aaron, Hank & Dick Schaap, *Hank Aaron: My Life in Pictures*, Total Sports and Major League Baseball Properties, Inc., Berkeley, California, 1999.

Aaron, Hank & Lonnie Wheeler, *I Had a Hammer,* HarperPaperbacks, a Division of HarperCollins Publishing, New York, *1991.*

Atlanta Braves Illustrated, Atlanta Braves Public Relations Department, Stein Printing Company, Atlanta, 1966.

The Atlanta Constitution, Atlanta, Georgia, articles, "Mathews First 30-Homer Cracker Since Les Burge," by Furman Bisher, page 7, August 28, 1950, "A Minor Legend: Ben Geraghty Dies…A Major League Dream Unfulfilled," by Charles Roberts, page 34, June 19, 1963, "Braves Christen Stadium, Whip Tigers," by Bill Clark, page 12, April 10, 1965; "Pittsburgh Team Practices 'Handshake' Ritual: Stadium Impresses Bucs' Clemente," by Al Thomy and "Willie's Wallop Surprised Him: 'Never Thought It Would Go,' Says Buc's 13th Inning Hero," by Charlie Roberts, page 42, April 13, 1966; "Attendance Puzzles Braves: The Chase Draws Ghosts," page 59, September 19, 1973 and "Eddie 'Cool,'" by Wayne Minshew, page 48, April 8, 1974; "There's Hope: Braves' PR Director Bob Hope Is Getting Ulcers Over Aaron," by Norman Arey, page 82, April 7, 1974; "Splat!: Irate Aaron Smacks Writer With Strawberries," by Charlie Roberts, page 33, July 24, 1974; "Jesse James Rides Again," by Gene Tharpe, page 5, April 19, 1976; "Hot Dog! Love That Grub," page 49, August 5, 1978; "Sports A.M.: Angels Release Ralph Garr," page 70, June 8, 1980; "Lost and found: Garr would like to find a spot in baseball," by Mike Luck, page 48, February 26, 1984; "Braves release 42-year-old Darrell Evans," by Joe Strauss, page 87, April 5, 1990; "Mother of Henry Aaron dies," by Associated Press, page D6, April 9, 2008 and "Honorin' Hank," page 52, April 9, 2014.

The Atlanta Constitution, Play Ball Atlanta Braves, special Atlanta Braves section, Atlanta, Georgia, April 9, 1968.

The Atlanta Journal-Constitution webpage: https://www.ajc.com/, article, "Capra: Aaron's home run ball should have been his," by I.J. Rosenberg, March 31, 2016.

The Atlanta Journal and Constitution magazines, "Atlanta Stadium Issue," Section 2, April 4, 1965; and "Atlanta Braves Issue," Section 2, April 10, 1966.

Austin American-Stateman (Austin, Texas), article, "Horsehide to Cowhide: Baseball Changes," by Steve Jacobson, *Newsday,* page 38, March 22, 1974.

'Babe,' the One and Only, Delmar Watson, editor, Images of the Past, Inc., Vintage Sports Photographs, Hollywood, California, 1992.

Bibliography

Ballparks web page, https://ballparks.com/, statistics, "Atlanta-Fulton County Stadium," by Munsey & Suppes.

Baseball Almanac web page, https://www.baseball-almanac.com/, lists, "All Century Team," "Hank Aaron: 1973 Game by Game Batting Logs," "Hank Aaron Home Runs," and "Hank Aaron Stats."

Baseball Reference web page, https://baseball-reference.com/, statistics, Dusty Baker, career player and managerial summary.

Baseball Visible web page: https://baseballvisible.com/, article, "What Does WAR Mean in Baseball?" by Johnny Alvin, May 18, 2023.

The Birmingham Post-Herald (Birmingham, Alabama), article, "Hank Aaron: up from obscurity: the star as a black activist," by Ira Berkow, NEA, page 13, August 17, 1973.

Bleacher Report web page: https://bleacherreport.com/, article, "Remembering the Day Hank Aaron Broke Babe Ruth's Home Run Record," by Zachary D. Rymer, April 7, 2014.

The Bradenton Herald (Bradenton, Florida), articles, "Aaron, Kuhn end 'feud,'" Associated Press, page 25, February 16, 1980; and "Who Led Braves in HRs? Aaron? No – Johnson," by Bill Lyon, Knight Newspapers, page 14, April 20, 1974.

Braves 1974 Scorebook, Official Atlanta Braves Program, Atlanta Braves Public Relations Department, Williams Printing Company, Atlanta, Ga., 1974.

Braves Magazine, Henry Louis Aaron Special Edition, article, "I Can Still Remember the Swing," by John Holland, Professional Sports Publications, New York, N.Y., page 19, 2021.

Bryant, Howard, *The Last Hero: A Life of Henry Aaron*, Pantheon Books, New York, New York.

The Chicago Tribune, (Chicago, Illinois), articles, "Ernie Banks Says," by Ernie Banks, page 61, August 22, 1969, and "I may run bases backwards – Hank," by John Husar, page 49, April 5, 1974.

The Courier News (Bridgewater, New Jersey), article, "Hank Aaron Day at Shea," by John Belis, page 29, July 9, 1973.

Cox, Randy, *A Baby Boomer's Guide to Collecting Comic Books and Baseball Cards*, Baby Boomer Book Publishing, Stone Mountain, Georgia, 2004.

Crater, Paul, *Baseball in Atlanta*, Arcadia Publishing, Charleston, South Carolina, 2007.

The Daily Herald (Provo, Utah), article, "For Hank Aaron: Pen Mightier Than the Bat," United Press International, page 8, January 22, 1974.

The Daily Item (Port Chester, New York), article, "Charlie Grimm compares: Ruth and Aaron were alike in many ways," by Will Grimsley, the Associated Press, page 25, April 9, 1974.

Davidson, Donald & Jesse Outlar, *Caught Short*, Bantam/Pathfinder Publishers, New York, January 1, 1983.

Democrat and Chronicle (Rochester, New York), article, "Aaron's awaiting word from owners on replacing Kuhn: home run king serious about commissioner job," Associated Press, Page 10, June 15, 1983.

The Durham Sun (Durham, North Carolina), articles, "Haddix Asks – 'What's so Historic About a Loss?'" by Joe Reichler, Associated Press, and "What Does a Guy Have to Do – to Win?: Harvey Haddix Hurls 12 Perfect Innings – But Loses Game in 13th," by Ed Wilks, Associated Press, Page 45, May 27, 1959.

Encyclopedia.com web page, https://www.encyclopedia.com/, article, "Aaron, Henry Louis ('Hank')."

ESPN web page, https://www.espn.com/, article, "Nationals pay Davey Johnson tribute," by Associated Press, September 22, 2013.

Fort Lauderdale News (Fort Lauderdale, Florida), article, "Aaron Chasing Ruth's Ghost," by Dick Young, reprinted from the *New York Daily News*, page 8, July 8, 1970.

The Gazette (Cedar Rapids, Iowa), article, "Garner found a home in Cedar Rapids: Baseball led 'terrific athlete" to Eastern Iowa," by Mark Dukes, page M8, August 20, 2017.

Georgia State University Signal, article, "There it Goes—600!" by Randy Cox, page 10, May 6, 1971.

Hank Aaron 715, Tentacle Books, New York, N.Y., and United Press International, New York, N.Y., *1974.*

Hank Aaron: A Tribute to the Hammer, *The Atlanta Journal-Constitution*, Triumph Publishing, Chicago, Illinois, 2021.

Bibliography

Hilderbrand, Chuck, *Sad Riddance, The Milwaukee Braves 1965 Season Amid a Sport and a World in Turmoil*, CreateSpace Independent Publishing Platform, 2016.

Hope, Bob, We Could've Finished Last Without You: An Irreverent Look at the Atlanta Braves, the Losingest Team in Baseball for the Past 25 Years, *Longstreet Press, Inc.*, Marietta, Georgia, 1991.

International Civil Rights Walk of Fame web page, https://www.nps.gov/, article, "Henry Louis 'Hank' Aaron."

The Ithaca Journal (Ithaca, New York), article, "Durocher Says Willie Mays Makes His Job a Lot Easier," by Joe Reichler, Associated Press, page 18, June 30, 1954.

Jensen, Don, *The Timeline History of Baseball*, Palgrave/MacMillan, 2005.

The Journal News (Hamilton, Ohio), articles, "Bill's Board," by Bill Moeller," "Hank hammers no. 714 but Reds win in 11th," by Bob Hunter, and "'Like money in the bank': Aaron, baseball's new monument, a marvel," by Gene Conard, page 15, April 5, 1974.

Klima, John, *Bushville Wins!* Thomas Dunne Books, St. Martin's Press, New York, 2012.

The Manhattan Mercury (Manhattan, Kansas), article, "Aaron idolized Jackie Robinson," by Associated Press, page 10, February 6, 1974.

The Memphis Press-Scimitar (Memphis, Tennessee), article, "'Mississippi Mudcat' Made His Own Mark in Majors: Babe's Last Homer Didn't Faze Guy Bush," by Scott Kent, page 20, April 20, 1978.

The Minneapolis Star (Minneapolis, Minnesota), article, "Billingham Scared: by tornado, not Hank," page 34, April 5, 1974.

MLB News web page, https://www.mlb.com/, articles, "9 Facts about Aaron you may not know: even more legends about Hammerin' Hank," by Michael Clair, January 22, 2021 and "Slinky to be inducted into Phillies Wall of Fame," by Larry Shenk, July 13, 2022.

The Naples Daily News (Naples, Florida), article, "Braves VP Fired over Suite Spat," by Milton Richman, United Press International, page 20, April 27, 1976.

Nashville Banner (Nashville, Tennessee), article, "'Most Thrilling Moment,' Says Jackie in Atlanta," by Joe Reichler, page 7, April 9, 1949.

National Baseball Hall of Fame web page, https://baseballhall.org/, articles, "Aaron's Legacy Preserved Through His Gift to the Hall," by Craig Muder; "Hank Aaron: Chasing the Dream," and "Hank Aaron, right fielder, Class of 1982, About Hank Aaron."

The Newark Advocate (Newark, Ohio), article, "Pete Rose pushing for 714," page 17, April 1, 1974.

New Castle News (Newcastle, Pennsylvania), article, "Sports parade: Hank Aaron—'a good soldier,'" by Milton Richman, United Press International, page 43, April 3, 1974.

Newsweek, article, "Hank Aaron Wastes No Time, "Vol. 83, Number 15, pages 72-74, April 15, 1974.

The New York Times web page, https://www.nytimes.com/, article, "Aaron Ties Babe Ruth with 714 Homer," by Dave Anderson, page 1, April 5, 1974.

The Oil City Derrick (Oil City, Pennsylvania), article, "Stargell Blames Cowhide for Decline in Home Runs," by Associated Press, page 10, March 1, 1975.

Orlando Evening Star (Orlando, Florida), article, "Hammerin' Hank Aaron: He's Worth Every Dime," by Hubert Mizell, Associated Press, page 7, March 9, 1972.

Palladium-Item (Richmond, Indiana), article, "Horsehide Shortage Brings Cowhide Baseball Approval," United Press International, page 12, May 5, 1973.

The Palm Beach Post (West Palm Beach, Florida), articles, "Aaron to Play on Kuhn's Order," by Larry Mlynczak, page 75, April 7, 1974 and "Aaron Relives Moment of 715th Home Run," by Associated Press, page 42, April 9, 1984.

Peters, Mark, *The Ultimate Hank Aaron Fun Fact and Trivia Book*, Perfect World Marketing, 2013.

The Philadelphia Inquirer (Philadelphia, Pennsylvania), article, "Giants Win Flat on 3-Run Homer by Thompson in 9th: One-Out Clout Off Branca Defeats Dodgers, 5-4; World Series Opens Today; Yanks' Reynolds Faces Koslo," by Stan Baumgartner, page 1, October 4, 1951.

Pittsburgh Post-Gazette (Pittsburgh, Pennsylvania), article, "Herbert Aaron, Sr.: Father of 3, including homer king Hank Aaron," by the Associated Press, page 41, May 24, 1998.

Bibliography

The Pittsburgh Press (Pittsburgh, Pennsylvania), article, "Many songwriters feel baseball's spell," by Bob Hertzel, *Pittsburgh Press*, page 73, May 14, 1989.

Plimpton, George, One for the Record: The Inside Story of Hank Aaron's Chase for the Home Run Record, *Little, Brown & Company*, New York, N.Y., April 26, 2016.

Poynter web page, https://www.poynter.org/, article, "Opinion: Remembering the Legendary Vin Scully," by Tom Jones, August 4, 2022.

The Press Gazette (Hillsboro, Ohio), article, "Aaron Back on Home Field," Associated Press, page 8, April 8, 1974.

Press and Sun-Bulletin (Binghamton, New York), articles, "Jackie May Become Baseball's Joe Louis," and "Robinson Is Expected to Be Dodger Star: He Faces Terrific Pressure," by Oscar Fraley, United Press, page 24, April 11, 1947.

The Press Telegram (Long Beach, California), article, "Al Downing: 'Aaron is going 0-for-4 against me,'" by Gordon Verrell, page 23, April 8, 1974.

The Raleigh Register (Beckley, West Virginia), article, "They're Out to See Aaron, Not Ford," by Rick Van Sant, United Press International, page 21, April 3, 1974.

The Republic (Columbus, Indiana), articles, "Billingham 'Knew' by Aaron's Swing," by United Press International, page 17, April 5, 1974 and "Hank Aaron 715, Bowie Kuhn 0," by United Press International, page 12, April 9, 1974.

Reviewing the Brew web page: https://reviewingthebrew.com/, article, "Jackie Robinson, Hank Aaron, and the Legacy of Race in Baseball," by Colin Bennett, January 31, 2013.

The Ringer web page, https://www.ringer.com/, article, "The Staggering Greatness of Hank Aaron, by the Numbers," by Zach Kram, January 22, 2021.

The Sacramento Bee (Sacramento, California), articles, "Report Has Oriole Owner Assuring Players Club Will Stay," page 22, March 2, 1975 and "Memories go tumbling with Atlanta Stadium," Bee News Services, page 34, August 3, 1997.

The Sheboygan Press (Sheboygan, Wisconsin), article, "Braves Bury 'Chokeup' Charges, by Chuck Capaldo, Associated Press, page 22, September 24, 1957.

Sidney Daily News (Sidney, Ohio), articles, "Aaron Smashes 714th Homer But Reds Win in 11," by Jerry Turner, and "Ruth Appeared When Nation Needed a Hero," United Press International, page 8, April 5, 1974.

Sports Collectors Daily web page, https://www.sportscollectorsdaily.com/, article, "Collecting Hank Aaron 715th Home Run Memorabilia," by Rich Mueller, April 8, 2014.

Sports Illustrated, article, "End of the Glorious Ordeal," by Ron Fimrite, Vol. 40, Number 15, pages 20-23, April 15, 1974.

Sports Illustrated, The Hammer: The Best of Hank Aaron from the Pages of *Sports Illustrated*, articles, "Hank Becomes a Hit," pages 39-43, August 18, 1969, "The First Frontier," pages 45-51, May 25, 1970, and "The Torturous Road to 715," pages 55-64, May 28, 1973, all by William Leggett; "Men With a Yen for the Fences," by Dick Young, pages 105-112, November 11, 1974; and "One for the Ages," by Ron Fimrite, pages 141-143, September 19, 1994.

Stanton, Tom, *Hank Aaron and the Home Run That Changed America*, HarperCollins Publishers, New York, 2004.

Stewart, Mark and Mike Kennedy, *How the Media Made Henry Aaron Hammering Hank,* The Lyons Press, Guilford, Connecticut, 2006.

The Sunday News (Lancaster, Pennsylvania), article, "Henry Aaron and the Great Chase," by Associated Press, page 35, April 14, 1974.

Tampa Bay Times (St. Petersburg, Florida), articles, "T. Aaron Faces Challenge, Too," the Best of Milt Richman, page 47, June 22, 1973, and "An Honest Cop Returns the Ball," by Buddy Martin, *St. Petersburg Times* Sports Editor, page 45, April 5, 1974.

The Terre Haute Tribune (Terre Haute, Indiana), article, "Every Time Henry Hits One Away It's Mother's Day for Mrs. Aaron," by Associated Press, page 11, May 11, 1971.

The Valley Times-News (Lanett, Alabama), article, "Aaron Swats No. 715 to Break Ruth's Record," by Randy Cox, page 7, April 9, 1974.

The Vincennes Sun-Commercial (Vincennes, Indiana), article, "Hank Aaron Snubs Award Presentation Because of Kuhn," by Hal Bock, Associated Press, page 11, January 29, 1980.

Warren Times-Mirror and Observer (Warren, Pennsylvania), article, "For Monte Irvin: Hall of Fame Doors Open," by Associated Press, page 9, February 8, 1973.